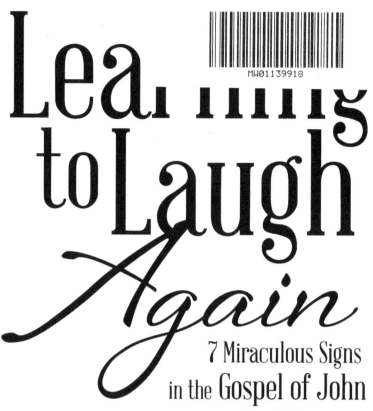

Learning to Laugh Again

7 Miraculous Signs
in the Gospel of John
That Point to the
Smiling Face
of Jesus

Learning to Laugh Again

7 Miraculous Signs
in the Gospel of John
That Point to the
Smiling Face
of Jesus

Rev. Dr. Marshall L. Hoffman

REDEMPTION
PRESS

Published by Redemption Press, PO Box 427, Enumclaw, WA 98022

Toll Free (844) 2REDEEM (273-3336)

Redemption Press is honored to present this title in partnership with the author. The views expressed or implied in this work are those of the author. Redemption Press provides our imprint seal representing design excellence, creative content, and high quality production.

ISBN 13: 978-1-68314-233-1
978-1-68314-234-8 (ePub)
978-1-68314-235-5 (Mobi)

Library of Congress Catalog Card Number: 2017937753

Dedication

To my Boss, a Jewish carpenter
whose happy heart and radiant disposition inspired this book.

Also, to believers on the path of faith who have laid aside their
garments of gladness in the rigors of growing older.

Table of Contents

Introduction

The path of holy humor is like an obstacle course. Every turn presents new problems that may temporarily defeat us in our quest. We need not be permanently defeated, however, because of our miracle-working Savior.

As we struggle to maintain a lifestyle of good cheer, we quickly discover that a sanctified sense of humor requires more power than we possess in our own natural capacities. How do we obtain such power? The theme of this book is: there is sufficient power in the miracles of Christ, and the Christ of miracles, to enable us to live in the spirit of holy hilarity.

> A sanctified sense of humor requires more power than we possess in our own natural capacities.

In the following pages I will narrow our attention to the seven signs of the Gospel of John. They are like signposts, pointing beyond themselves to the Fountain from which streams of joy flow. In addition to the seven signs, I will point out the resurrection as the sign of signs and the consummation of our rejoicing. For good measure, I include the postscript John

> A sign is never intended to point to itself but to something greater than itself.

provides in chapter twenty-one. Scholars think it may have been added later, as an appendix, to clarify a misunderstanding that had arisen in the early church. It provides a fascinating way for us to bring our study of a merry heart to a fitting climax.

A miracle may exist for its own sake and for the startling impact it may create upon the minds of those who witness it. A sign is never intended to point to itself but to something greater beyond itself. Alan Richardson says:

> Throughout the New Testament the word "wonders" is never used without the word "signs." It is as though the New Testament writers were unwilling to emphasize the miracles as mere wonders but desire rather to point to their meaning, their significance as signs. They are not interested in Jesus as wonder-worker, but as the expected Messiah of God.[1]

In this book, I have no interest in the miracles for their own sake. My consistent aim will be to go beyond each miracle to its underlying message. We will discover a pattern. The significance of each sign is to point away from itself to the Lord of glory who is working in our lives. As we follow each sign to its ultimate destination, an unveiling of the glory of Jesus, we will encounter a power that will lift our hearts in ever-laughing life.

> In the unveiling of the glory of Jesus, we will encounter a power that will lift our hearts in ever-laughing life.

---

[1]   Alan Richardson, The Miracle-Stories of the Gospels (London: SCM Press Ltd., 1941), 46.

Obviously, these seven signs were not intended to beautify the path or call attention to their own qualities. They were intended to lead us safely to our destination. Our purpose is not to look to them, but through them, to the greater reality standing behind them. Thus, as we come to the first sign, we are not concerned for the wine itself. Was it unfermented grape juice or what? All such questions lead us far astray. The important thing is to see the power of God taking the thin and watery elements of our lives and transforming them into the wine of joy.

> Our ultimate destination is a merry heart and the smiling face of Jesus.

Traveling the highways, one of the road signs we may look for is the one that says, "Scenic Route." We like to follow that sign because it promises beautiful scenery as we travel along. Each one of the signs in John's Gospel is a scenic route that opens vistas of the glory of Christ and the majesty of His being.

Other signs read, "Merge to the Right." They challenge us to merge our thinking with mainstream Christianity. We serve a living Savior, a Christ of miracles, who is working in our world and in our lives as He worked in these ancient wonders. They point to His never-failing ability to take our propensity for pessimism and transform it into overflowing joy.

Beginning with the water turned to wine, each miracle will take us to the next level in our quest. So buckle up; let's follow the signs to our ultimate destination of a merry heart and the smiling face of Jesus.

"Get a Transfer"

If you are on the Gloomy Line,
get a transfer.

If you're inclined to fret and pine,
get a transfer.
Get off the track of doubt and gloom,
get on the Sunshine Track—
there's room—
get a transfer.
If you're on the Worry Train,
get a transfer.
You must not stay there and complain,
get a transfer.
The Cheerful cars are passing
through,
And there's a lot of room for you— get a transfer.
If you're on the Grouchy Track,
get a transfer
Just take a Happy Special back,
get a transfer.
Jump on the train and pull the rope,
that lands you at the station Hope—Get a transfer.

Hampton H. Sewell[2]

> **It's easy to get sidetracked onto grouchiness and grumpiness.**

It's so easy to get off the track of joy and gladness and get sidetracked onto grouchiness and grumpiness. This often breeds doctrinal divisions. Why, even members of the same denomination can reject each other.

I heard about a well-known Southern Baptist pastor who was resolute in his doctrinal

---

[2]   Hampton H. Sewell, 1874–1937, originally published in Songs for Jesus, 1925, quoted by Cal and Rose Samra, Holy Humor, Inspiration Wit & Cartoons, 36.

beliefs, yet he had a reputation for reaching out in kindness and compassion to those in distress. One day he was called upon to talk a man off a ledge who was threatening to jump. He leaned out the window of the skyscraper and yelled, "Don't jump!"

The man replied, "I've got nothing to live for."

The pastor asked, "What about your family?"

"I've got none," the man on the ledge said. After a long pause, the pastor exclaimed, "I'm sure we could be friends, I bet we have a lot in common."

"I doubt that," said the man teetering on the edge.

"Well, do you believe in God?"

"Yes," said the man.

"See," says the Southern Baptist minister, "we have that in common." He continued, "Are you a Christian . . . a Baptist by any chance?"

"Why, yes. I am," replied the man, with a look of encouragement on his face.

"What kind of a Baptist are you?" inquired the pastor. "Southern, Conservative, American, or General Assembly of Regular Baptists, or maybe Seventh Day Baptists?"

"No sir," the distraught man said, "I am a Northern Baptist."

The pastor shut the window and said, "In that case, jump you heretic!"

———

May this book help you transfer to the "glory train." Jesus put it best when He said: "When you fast, do not put on a gloomy look as the hypocrites do" (Matt. 6:16). St. Teresa of Avila (AD 1582) frequently prayed: "From somber, serious, sullen saints, save us, O Lord. Lord hear our prayer."

ONE

The Beginning of Laughter

The First Sign, Turning Water into Wine, Makes the Wedding Party Fine, a Fun Time

On the third day a wedding took place at Cana in Galilee. Jesus' mother was there, and Jesus and his disciples had also been invited to the wedding. When the wine was gone, Jesus' mother said to him, "They have no more wine."

"Woman, why do you involve me?" Jesus replied. "My hour has not yet come."

His mother said to the servants, "Do whatever he tells you."

Nearby stood six stone water jars, the kind used by the Jews for ceremonial washing, each holding from twenty to thirty gallons.

Jesus said to the servants, "Fill the jars with water"; so they filled them to the brim. Then he told them, "Now draw some out and take it to the master of the banquet." They did so, and the master of the banquet tasted the water that had been turned into wine. He did not realize where it had come from, though the servants who had drawn the water knew. Then he called the bridegroom aside and said, "Everyone brings out the choice wine first and then the cheaper wine after the guests have had too much to drink; but you have saved the best till now." What Jesus did here in Cana of Galilee was the first of the signs through which he revealed his glory; and his disciples believed in him. (John 2:1–11)

Natural, Supernatural, or a Blending of Both?

> The parable of the sower is the key understanding the essence of holy humor and how it works in our lives.

Adrian Rodgers quotes Dr. G. Campbell Morgan as saying: "Every parable Jesus spoke was a miracle of instruction and every miracle Jesus performed was a parable for instruction."[3] As there is a miraculous element in the parables, there is a parabolic dimension to the miracles. It is helpful to see this intimate relationship between miracles and parables. R. C. Trench ingeniously suggests there is a correlation between the first parable Jesus uttered and the first miracle he performed in Cana of Galilee. "This beginning of miracles is as truly an introduction to all other miracles which Christ wrought, as the parable of the Sower to all other parables which He spoke."[4]

The Gospel of Mark indicates that understanding the parable of the sower is the key to understanding all the parables (Mark 4:13). In like manner, this beginning of signs is the key to all the miracles and the key to understanding the essence of holy humor and how it works in our lives.

In trying to explain away the miracle, some have suggested there may have been residues of wine left in the stone jars and when water was added, it resulted in a diluted mixture: not wine, but better than

---

[3] Adrian Rogers, *Believe in Miracles but Trust in Jesus* (Wheaton: Crossway Books, A Division of Good News Publishers, 1997), 12.

[4] Richard Chenevix Trench, *Notes on the Miracles of our Lord* (Grand Rapids: Wm. B. Eeerdmans Publishing Company, 1951), 63.

The power of laughter has the capacity to transform natural law.

plain water. However, stone jars were used exclusively for water and for religious ceremonies of purification that were required by Mosaic law. Precious wine was stored in wine skins.

What we have in our passage of Scripture is not a natural mingling but a supernatural transformation. That is our understanding of joy. Trench says a happy heart is more like "a turning of the water of earth into the wine of heaven; an ennobling of the common, and a transmuting of the mean."[5] Such transformation is in part natural, but it transcends nature. The power of laughter has the capacity, we believe, to even transform natural law, lifting it to its highest potential, in a way that goes beyond our understanding or our ability to explain. The laws of nature are not suspended or violated in the miracles of Jesus. Rather, they are liberated to perform in ways unknown to us at our present stage of knowledge.

The miracle of merriment works on this same principle. Our natural state is suspicion and unbelief. By nature, we are prone to pessimism. Like the Old Testament people of God during their wilderness wanderings, we are easily mired in the mud of murmuring and mumbling. No matter what God does for us, we can find some grounds for grouchy grumbling.

But, when the Word becomes flesh and incarnates Himself in the stuff of our humanity, we are liberated from grumpiness in a way that is truly miraculous. It does not violate natural law; it lifts it to its highest potential.

I heard about a Sunday school teacher who was sharing with her class the good news,

Like the people of God during their wilderness wanderings, we are easily mired in the mud of murmuring and mumbling.

---

[5] Trench, 63.

| The natural is accelerated by the supernatural. | "God loves us even when we are grumpy." One child spoke up and said, "Not only that, teacher, God loves us even when we are Happy and Sleepy and Dopey and Sneezy and Dock and Bashful." Now that's the whole, seven-fold gospel in a nursery rhyme. |

The natural process of turning water into wine is going on all around us. It takes months for the grapevine to take in water through its root system, and with the energy of the sun, turn it into the fruit of the vine. It takes more time to harvest the fruit, and through another natural process of fermentation, to produce the finished product. All of this was done instantaneously and miraculously by the power of our Savior.

Such acceleration is what happens when we experience spiritual renewal. There's something about a fresh filling of the Spirit that causes things to move very quickly. Spiritual gifts that may have lain dormant for many years spring to new life and vitality when we experience the reality of this first sign. A kind of spiritual photosynthesis occurs whereby the light of truth and the water of the Word produce the fruit of joy on the branch of our relationship with Christ, which is the source of our sanctified sense of humor. In a vintage year of renewal, that can all come about very quickly as the natural is accelerated by the supernatural. When our Lord is in charge and the Spirit is flowing freely, it's amazing how rapidly it all comes to fruition.

Violation or Acceleration?

Rather than a suspension, this concept of an acceleration of natural law in explaining some miracles is very helpful to certain people. Some people who have been schooled in critical thinking and the scientific method find it very difficult to conceive of God setting aside natural law in performing a supernatural event. For them, it seems like God is violating His own nature to abrogate natural law that He established to maintain an orderly universe. A better approach for them is the one we see illustrated in this first sign. Colin Brown says, "Physical miracles may be rendered intelligible by suggesting an acceleration of natural processes in accordance with laws unknown to us."[6] Does it seem strange that what takes nature months to accomplish, the God of nature can do in an

> The first sign points back to the past and connects us to Moses and his first sign to Pharaoh.

instant? The One who is the True Vine, the Water of Life and the Light of the world can take the carbon dioxides of this world's waste and turn them into the pure oxygen of love. He does this in the twinkling of an eye when we surrender our lives to Him. It is a sudden transformation that is truly miraculous to those who experience it.

The Glory of the Prophetic

The eleventh verse tells us that Jesus "revealed his glory" in this first miraculous sign. Part of that glory must have been the instantaneous nature of the miracle. What was poured into pots as water was poured out as fine wine. Such a sudden change is indeed glorious. In addition, there is a resplendent glory in the prophetic significance of this first sign, for those who have eyes to see. It points back to the past and connects us to Moses and his first sign to Pharaoh. Long before the advent of Jesus, Deuteronomy 18:18 had been regarded as a Messianic promise. God is speaking to Moses: "I will raise up for them a prophet like you from among their brothers; I will put my words in his mouth,

---

[6]   Colin Brown, *Miracles and the Critical Mind* (Grand Rapids: Wm. B. Eeerdmans Publishing Company, 1984), 113.

> Christ appeared to transform the thin, watery elements of legalistic religion into the richness of spiritual renewal.

and he will tell them everything I command him." A prophet like Moses? How were Jesus and Moses similar to each other? Moses' first miracle was the changing of the Nile River into blood. This began a process of deliverance which ultimately led to the freeing of the children of Israel from the slavery of Egypt. Our Lord's first miracle was the changing of water into wine. Wine is often used in the New Testament as a symbol for blood. This miracle began a process that led ultimately to the deliverance of mankind from the slavery of sin and the bondage of guilt. In this first sign God is signifying that the one like unto Moses has come. Thus, there is a striking resemblance between Moses and Jesus in regard to the beginning of their miraculous signs that led to liberation and deliverance.

In its prophetic significance, it not only points back to the past and the prophet Moses, it reflects upon the reality of first century Judaism. "They have no wine," sounds like the heart cry of a nation chafing under the cruel yoke of law. A complicated "thou-shalt-not" system left people tied in knots of negative prohibitions. Christ appeared to transform the thin, watery elements of legalistic religion into the richness of a new birth of spiritual renewal. "Judaism is but the water of purification from which Christ makes the wine of eternal life."[7] Just as Moses appeared in response to the heart cry of his people who suffered under a cruel yoke of bondage, so Christ appeared because the Father heard our cry and sent us a Savior.

> "They have no wine," is the heart cry of religion without joy.

---

[7]   Richardson, 122.

There is a sense in which the prophetic insights of this first miracle can also be applied to contemporary Christianity. "They have no wine," is the heart cry of religion without joy. How easily we go through the motions of religious observance, but the inner meaning and vitality run out. We continue to go through the mechanics of what tradition requires, but we know not why. We would do well to apply this first miracle not only to the religious life of Jesus' day, but to our own day and time. When we slip into ruts of the routine, where sounds of laughter are seldom heard, it could be said our wine has run dry. We need a miracle.

> Moses' first miracle was a plague. Christ's first miracle was a blessing, not a curse.

While appreciating the similarities, we must not fail to observe the great disparity. Moses' first miracle was a plague. Turning the water into blood made it undrinkable. It signified the wrath and judgment of God upon the Egyptian oppressors and their unjust oppression. Christ's first miracle was a blessing, not a curse. It pictured joy and gladness, not wrath and judgment. It brought added enjoyment to an already happy occasion and kept the wedding festival from coming to a premature conclusion. In this we see a clear picture of our Lord's mission. And not only His mission, we see a glorious reflection of His bright and sunny disposition, His radiant personality with which he was blessed above all men, and with which He blessed others.

It is true; the Bible describes him as "a Man of sorrows and acquainted with grief" (Isaiah 53:3 NKJV). Through the incarnation, He became acquainted with our grief; our sorrow He took upon himself.

The book of Hebrews informs us the Father has anointed Him with the "oil of gladness" above all others (Heb. 1:9 NKJV). His is the sunniest disposition, the cheeriest attitude that ever graced the pages of

His is the sunniest disposition, the cheeriest attitude. If some of that ever rubs off onto us, our water will be turned to the wine of holy hilarity.

history. If some of that ever rubs off onto us, our water will be turned to the wine of holy hilarity.

The life of the average Galilean was hard and dreary. For the most part they were fishermen and farmers who were heavily taxed by their Roman conquerors. As they scratched out a bare subsistence from the soil and the Sea of Galilee, their joys were few and far between. The one bright spot in an otherwise drab existence was an occasional wedding that might be the social event of the year. It could last a full week with everyone in the general vicinity coming and going in shifts. Toward the end of the week when the wine ran out, Jesus performed a miracle to save the host from embarrassment and to keep a happy, wholesome occasion from breaking up prematurely. He wanted the party to continue. Knowing him, I would expect He was having more fun than anyone else. I can picture him with His broad smile and an attitude of "let the good times roll."

Having come from the heart of God, Jesus knew intimately what would cause the joy bells of heaven to ring. "There will be more rejoicing in heaven over one sinner who repents than over ninety-nine righteous persons who do not need to repent" (Luke 15:7). The parable of the prodigal son amply illustrates this statement. When the prodigal returned after a long and tragic so-journ in the far country where he squandered his inheritance, his older brother (too often a picture of the upright who are uptight) was

He wanted the party to continue. I would expect He was having more fun than anyone else.

sullen and unforgiving. The father was delighted. As he said to his more responsible older son: "We had to celebrate and be glad, because this brother of yours was dead and is alive again; he was lost and is found" (Luke 15:32). While son number one remained outside, stewing in the juices of jealousy and resentment, son number two feasted on the fatted calf with his father and the servants. Do you want to inspire a party in heaven? Find the least, the last, the lost, and encourage them to return to the Father for forgiveness.

Jesus or John the Baptist?

What insight does this give us into His personality? It tells us Jesus was no frowning saint in the sanctimonious sense of the word. No wonder children were drawn to Him. The second verse informs us that Jesus was "invited" to the wedding feast. He was the kind of person you would want to invite because he wasn't a killjoy. He had a contagious spirit which brought people together and made it easier for them to laugh and talk. With Jesus there, many people were thinking, This is the best party I've been to in years; I wish it would last forever! Unfortunately, more difficult times were coming. As Jesus said to His mother, "My hour has not yet come" (John 2:4). He knew His hour of crucifixion was at hand. He couldn't escape His destiny even at a party. Nevertheless, Jesus did something special for it to continue a little longer. You mean to say, Jesus would use His special powers in such a way to keep a party going? The thought of that used to offend me, but now it delights me. It tells me that's the kind of person He is; and that's the kind of Person in whom I can believe. As verse eleven says, "His disciples believed in him." Isn't that

> Would Jesus use his special powers to keep a party going? That used to offend me, but now delights me.

We need the first sign to put us in touch with the real Jesus, not a distorted image from our heritage.

just like Him? That's why He is the source and the fountainhead of our praise. He comes not to bring a plague upon our houses, to take the blue out of our sky, the spring out of our steps, or the joy out of our hearts. As He said: "I have come that they might have life, and that they may have it more abundantly" (John 10:10 NKJV).

It is my contention that our Puritan roots (and there is immense good we have received from our Puritan forbearers) have caused us to misunderstand our Savior and cast him more in the role of John the Baptist. John was a great man. Jesus paid him the highest respect when He said, "Among those born of women there has not risen anyone greater than John the Baptist" (Matt. 11:11). Nevertheless, John was never intended to be our perfect pattern. John was a loner who lived an austere life of rugged asceticism in the desert. He punished his body with the coarse clothing of camel's hair and thundered the message of wrath and judgment on all who came to hear. He was not the kind of man you would likely invite to a neighborhood party unless you wanted to change it into a revival meeting. He was not the kind of person who could or would engage in social pleasantries. Yet, somehow, in our Puritan perceptions, we are always confusing John with Jesus, whereas they were as different as night and day. Let us honor John in his place as the forerunner of Christ, but let's remember that Jesus is our highest example. We need this first sign to put us in touch with the real Jesus, not a distorted image we may have received from our heritage.

The Christian Home

With all its prophetic significance and insights into the person of Jesus, this first sign points to some practical benefits our Lord would bring into our lives, especially in the area of marriage and the home. We never want to forget our Lord chose to begin His ministry of miracles at a wedding. I feel that is significant. It tells us the best place to experience the miracle of spiritual transformation is in the home.

While couples are forming their invitation list of relatives and friends, how thoughtless not to invite Jesus. Put Him at the top of your guest list and send him a personal invitation carried on wings of prayer. He is too much of a perfect gentleman to crash your party or barge in where He is not invited. But He is too much of a friend not to honor your invitation with His presence. And He'll do what no one else can. Pastors can repeat the time-honored vows, "For better or for worse, in sickness and in health, as long as we both shall live." But only the unity of His love can take two separate lives and mold them together until they become one. How important that He be there to work this great miracle. The unity candle can only symbolize, but he can finalize the mystery of two becoming one.

The best thing a couple can do is not only invite our Lord to their marriage but invite Him into their hearts and the home they would establish. The home is like a miniature solar system. Husband and wife have their proper orbits of privilege and responsibility. Children may come to establish additional orbits. What is at the center that is massive enough in meaning to hold it all together? At the beginning, couples think their physical attraction for each other will suffice. They tend to make each other the center of their world. But what happens when the honeymoon is over and people settle down to live ordinary lives? Sexual gratification is not sufficient in itself to hold people on course in the bond of holy matrimony. Only the Son of God is sufficient to be the center of our marital

> Only the unity of the love of Christ can take two separate lives and mold them together until they become one.

> Our romantic myth of "falling in love" is not a biblical concept.

solar system. Only the gravitational pull of His love is powerful enough to hold family members in their designed orbits.

That dangerous period just beyond the honeymoon stage is very vulnerable. When the "rocket's red glare, the bombs bursting in air" of their sexual passion has subsided, young couples may think they are no longer "in love." Our romantic myth of "falling in love" is not a biblical concept. We don't fall in love; we step into it by a wise decision and a sacred commitment. But people do fall in love with *love*. And the sooner they fall out the better. When we are no longer in love with love, we are free to love a person rather than a feeling or a function; we are free to step up to the next level of our relationship, beyond the honeymoon stage. On that level, "the way you make me feel," slips into the background and "the unique person you are" takes center stage.

Not only the solar system with Christ at the center, but the triangle with Christ at the apex, is a helpful metaphor for the Christian home. As wife and husband move toward the apex of their faith, they move toward each other. Finally, they become one in Him. The best thing any Christian couple can do in strengthening the ties that bind, is to draw near their Savior as they share their faith with each other and pray and read the Scriptures together. That family altar they have with each other is the apex of their oneness, as well as those morning or evening devotions.

> We don't fall in love; we step into it by a wise decision and a sacred commitment.

Absolutely Essential, but Simply Boring

Jesus specializes in turning water into wine, bringing zest and sparkle to the routine.

Water is absolutely essential to survival. One can live a lot longer without food than water. While so essential, it is nevertheless so colorless, odorless, and tasteless. Can you think of anything less exciting than drinking water? Sleeping with the same person, raising a family, pursuing a career, making a home: so many essentials can become thin and watery.

Jesus specializes in turning the water into wine, bringing zest and sparkle to that which has become routine. You need Him in your home and in your heart, especially when monotony begins to close in. Without the miracle of his transformation, it is doubly difficult to make marriage work over the long haul.

The Joy of Serving Others

There is a precious parenthesis in verse nine: "Though the servants who had drawn the water knew." What the governor of the feast and other dignitaries and guests did not know, the servants knew. Having filled the jars with water and carried it to the guests, they were in the best position to know what others were oblivious to. Yes, there are things you can know just by being in His service and serving others in His name. That's one of the best rewards of service. You are right there, in the best possible position, to know the wonderful details of how He is working in the lives of

One of the best rewards of service is you are in the best possible position to know the wonderful details of how He is working in the lives of people.

> Any time Christ is in control, the best is always *now*.

people. One of the most exciting things you can know throughout your career of serving Jesus is the reality of verse ten, "You have saved the best till now."

The festival coordinator, as we might call him, is literally dumbfounded! Not by the miracle; he was not even aware one had occurred. What amazed him was the strategy of the bridegroom. Put into the language of modern colloquialism, it might sound something like this: "Listen, old buddy, everybody knows you serve the good stuff first, while people's tastes are still tuned to appreciate the delicate flavor. Then, when their senses are somewhat numbed, you slip in the cheaper stuff, and they don't notice the difference. Well, what gives? You have kept the best vintage until now!"

The explanation is simple; any time Christ is in control the best is always *now*. Our Lord said, "I do not give to you as the world gives" (John 14:27). There is something profoundly different between the strategies of the world and the kingdom, which gives birth to a merry heart. The worldly plan is, "serve the good wine first." The world promises everything: pleasure, excitement, a thrill a minute, and for a while it seems to deliver. Then, when you are caught in the web of enticement, it reveals its red, hourglass underside, nature's symbol of the truth that time is running out. In the time that remains, things can only go from bad to worse.

A Sex Symbol Turned Sour

Marilyn Monroe is one of the most heartrending examples. She was lured by the bright lights of Hollywood that promised fame and fortune. And she made it big. Her name in lights could sell more tickets to more theaters than any other Hollywood star. She was sitting on top of the world, worshipped by men as the sex symbol of America. For a while it was good, very good. But then "the wine failed." She found herself detesting the very thing she was supposed to represent and feeling the phoniness of it all. More and more she resented being used as a commercial item to pad the pockets of a heartless industry that would discard her when she could no longer boost ratings and sell tickets. She wasn't loved as a person; she was exploited as a body. We all know the tragic ending.

> God replaces what time takes away with enduring spiritual qualities of maturity.

How different it is with Jesus. With Him the best is always *now*. But you say, how about all the energy, the vitality, and the youthfulness that the years take away from you? What time takes away, God more than replaces with depth of soul, with spiritual qualities of maturity that are so much more enduring.

Grapes are very perishable. They must be picked quickly before they spoil on the vines. But wine endures and a good vintage may even improve with age. Picture in your mind a vintner going down into the wine cellar for a famous label that has been aging over the years. The bottle may be dusty and circled with cobwebs. It doesn't look like much on the outside. But when the cork is withdrawn, it gives forth a full flavor and aroma which is a delight to those who sample it. Such aging brings it to the zenith of its fullness. Jesus says, "My Father is the vinedresser" (John 15:1 NKJV). He knows how to preserve and perfect those inner spiritual qualities which are enduring. The wisdom of Proverbs puts it so well: "The path of the righteous is like the first gleam of dawn, shining ever brighter till the full light of day" (Prov. 4:18). As we walk those paths of righteousness in His name, we expect that the sublime strategy we see unfolding in this first miracle will come back to bless us again and again with the realization that He has saved the best for now.

The Best Advice Anyone Could Give

> Draw out of your own experiences and share the water of life with some thirsty soul. Your water may become someone else's wine.

The best advice that anyone could receive is that which the blessed mother of our Lord gives in the context of this first miracle; "Do whatever he tells you." That word applies whether we are married, single, divorced, widowed, or whatever. If we are not Christian, we begin our Christian life by inviting Jesus to come and live His life through us. If we are already Christian, we seek to be filled to the "brim" with His delightful disposition. Following this sign, we seek a place of service where, in the words of verse eight, you can "draw some out and take it to" others. You can draw out of your own experiences and share the water of life with some thirsty soul. You may find your water becoming someone else's wine.

For those Spirit-filled Christians who are in an active place of service, this first sign has an additional word of advice: that we fulfill the role of intercessory prayer. Like the blessed mother of our Lord, we can go to Him on behalf of others who have no wine. We can intercede on their behalf. Perhaps the "hour has not yet come" for them to receive their miracle. But we can continue to lift them up until that hour comes, knowing God will use our petitions to accomplish His perfect will.

That is good guidance for us as we begin on the first level of holy humor. If He says, "Fill," let us "fill to the brim," with wholehearted

> Whatever He says, we must be prepared to implement in obedience.

30

obedience. If he says, "Draw," let us draw out of our resources of happiness and "take" that to others who "have no wine." Perhaps it is we who have no wine. We need to confess our condition and invite Him to come and make the difference. We can be sure our Christ of miracles will speak to our consciences from this first sign. The more we get into it, the clearer His voice will be. Whatever He says, we must be prepared to implement in obedience.

> Because He lives, this first miracle can be reduplicated in our lives today.

A Day of Resurrection

This first sign occurred on the "third day." We assume that means the third day since the five (Andrew and Peter, Philip, Nathanael and John) had become followers of Jesus. What if it has a deeper significance? On the third day of the week of creation, continents arose from their watery graves and dry land appeared and began to be covered with the greenery of life. Jesus arose on the third day. This first miracle assures us we too can have a third-day experience. We can know the power of His resurrection, and our barren lives can be clothed with new meaning. Because He lives, the meaning of this first miracle lives and can be reduplicated in our lives today. What a springboard for launching into a lifestyle of laughter.

When did the transformation actually occur? While the water was being poured into the stone receptacles? While it sat there waiting to be utilized? Or, as it was drawn out and carried to others? We are not told. In my view, the miracle of transformation should not be associated with water sitting passively in stone containers but with the process of distributing it to others in need of refreshment.

What a lesson for us! There is a transformation of joy within us as we draw out of our own experiences and carry that to others in acts of service, offering to them the insights of the gospel and the pleasures we have found in serving Jesus. As we take Jesus at His word and act upon it, wonderful things can happen. We can find ourselves laughing with the One who is "anointed with the oil of gladness" (Heb. 1:9 NKJV). His inspired words are a wellspring of joy within us. As He said: "I have told you this so that my joy may be in you and that your joy may be complete" (John 15:11).

> There is a transformation of joy within us as we draw out of our experiences and carry that to others.

TWO

The Continuation of Laughter

The Second Sign: a Word of Good Cheer That Inspires a Smile and Transcends Time.

Once more he visited Cana in Galilee, where he had turned the water into wine. And there was a certain royal official whose son lay sick at Capernaum. When this man heard that Jesus had arrived in Galilee from Judea, he went to him and begged him to come and heal his son, who was close to death.

"Unless you people see signs and wonders," Jesus told him, "you will never believe."

The royal official said, "Sir, come down before my child dies."

"Go," Jesus replied, "your son will live."

The man took Jesus at his word and departed. While he was still on the way, his servants met him with the news that his boy was living. When he inquired as to the time when his son got better, they said to him, "Yesterday, at one in the afternoon, the fever left him."

Then the father realized that this was the exact time at which Jesus had said to him, "Your son will live." So he and his whole household believed.

This was the second sign Jesus performed after coming from Judea to Galilee.
(John 4:46–54)

G. Campbell Morgan said, "The remarkable thing about this second sign is that it was the operation of power at a distance, and the healing of the boy was not wrought by any physical contact with Christ at all."[8] William Taylor said, "What he intended to teach this man was that he, who had life in himself, could restore life at a distance as easily by the word of his power, as . . . by personal application."[9] Likewise, there is something about the gladness of a happy heart that transcends time and puts us in contact with the One who is "with us always, even unto the end of the world" (Matt. 28:20 NKJV).

The nobleman was quite probably connected with the court of Herod Antipas. There have been some ingenious attempts to connect him with Chuza, whom Luke mentions as the husband of Joanna, one of the godly women who ministered to the Lord out of their substance. He is described by Luke as "the manager of Herod's household" (Luke 8:3). He had a very responsible position as the steward of Herod's estate. Through his wife's direct experience of Jesus' healing power, he might have been favorably impressed by His growing reputation. Other attempts have been made to link him with Manaen, who is mentioned in Acts as one of the "prophets and teachers" who had a leading role in the church at Antioch in the years that followed the death and resurrection of Jesus. Manaen "had been brought up with Herod the tetrarch," and may have been a foster brother (Acts 13:1). None of these ingenious attempts at identification is important except to note that, as a man

---

8   G. Campbell Morgan, *The Great Physician* (New York: Fleming H. Revell Company, 1937), 82.
9   William M. Taylor, *The Miracles of our Saviour* (New York: Doubleday, Doran and Company, Inc., 1928), 52.

of authority who served under the king, he was accustomed to having his own way.

Word of mouth travels fast in all directions. It didn't take long for a high-ranking official whose son was critically ill in Capernaum, some twenty miles away, to hear of Jesus' return to Cana of Galilee. The great Galilean prophet was back in town. People were still talking about what happened the first time. Six empty stone water pots, holding up to thirty gallons each, were filled with water. There was a wedding party going on, without a drop of

> The great Galilean prophet was back in town. People were still talking about what happened the first time.

wine and an abundance of nearly two hundred gallons of water. The next minute there was enough wine for the whole village for the foreseeable future.

Are you like me? I find this situation highly entertaining and humorous. Truly our Savior has a delightful sense of humor! I mean, there it was, suddenly, out of nowhere, multiple gallons of the best wine you have ever tasted.

In case you were wondering, the nobleman didn't bring camels loaded with water for a repeat of that first miracle. He brought a heart that was rent by sorrow. Driven by desperation, he left the bedside of his dying son to seek the help of the miracle worker. Leaving early in the morning he traveled the distance between Capernaum and Cana, arriving at the seventh hour, about 1:00 p.m. The forty-seventh verse says, as soon as he found Jesus, he "begged him to come and heal his son, who was close to death." Obviously, his son meant more to him than anything else in the world. That's why he made this venture. Yet, Jesus didn't budge an inch!

Amazing Reluctance

> Was Jesus testing the father's limited faith so it might break forth onto a new level of joyfulness?

I find that rather amazing! When invited, He attended the wedding in Cana of Galilee. If He would go to a wedding to add gladness to an already happy occasion, why wouldn't He go with this grieving father to banish sadness from a home darkened by the shadow of death? Verse forty informs us that when the Samaritans urged him to extend his visit with them, he stayed two days longer than He had planned. Now, this desperate father literally pleads for Jesus to come to his home and our Lord refuses to go. Why? Could it be to test the father's limited faith, that it might transcend its limitations and break forth onto a new level of joyfulness?

Obviously, the father in our Scripture had some kind of faith. He couldn't leave the bedside of his boy at this critical hour unless he believed there was a core of reality behind the growing reputation of Jesus. If such a noted healer could only come to his town, enter his house and place his miracle-working hands on his child, the fever might leave and the son survive. He had some kind of faith, but it seemed to be limited to the physical presence of Jesus.

We meet people all the time, who have no problem believing Jesus did all the signs and wonders that are recorded in the four Gospels. Many of these same people believe that when Jesus comes again He will do even greater things. If Jesus made himself visibly present in one of our worship services, wonderful things would happen. But, as we know, He is absent,

> His Word reaches across the galaxies and brings miracles of healing.

seated at the right hand of the Father in heaven. Therefore, don't expect anything miraculous to happen. But, must Jesus be physically present for something miraculous to happen? Miracle of miracles, His power transcends space and time. His Word reaches across the galaxies and brings miracles of healing.

Symptoms of Limited Faith

Our faith may be just as limited as the father's in our passage of Scripture. A symptom of our limited faith is our inclination to make a distinction between various kinds of illness. If the illness is psychosomatic in nature, that is, the result of mind and emotions on the body, something marvelous might happen. But, if it's an organic disease, like cancer, that is beyond the function of faith. Many of us are deeply influenced by the insights of modern psychology upon theology, and it has put barriers around our believing.

Others take the doctrinal position that the age of miracles ended with the apostles. When Jesus and the apostles walked the earth, there was no completed canon of Scripture. Signs and wonders were needed to persuade people and to strengthen the credibility of the message and the messenger. But now that the message is fully recorded, miracles are no longer needed. Thus, our traditions, our expectations, our past experiences, our theological positions and our cultural conditioning all tend to limit our capacity to believe and put parameters around our faith.

Our world view and how we conceive of the universe may also limit our capacity to believe. There are those with a mechanistic

> Our traditions, expectations, past experiences, theological positions, and our cultural conditioning limit our capacity to believe.

> **Without testing, our faith can never expand beyond its present borders.**

view of reality who see the world as a closed system of cause and effect. Everything is governed by natural law, which brooks no interference and makes the thought of anything miraculous seem absurd. Throughout the nineteenth century, Newtonian physics was interpreted in such a way as to give support to this mechanistic theory. The theory of relativity has opened up fields of science to a much more dynamic understanding of how our universe works. Laws of cause and effect are not nearly so rigid and predictable. In the spiritual sense, we have more encouragement from the scientific community to keep ourselves open to the possibility of the miraculous.

How can we break out of our boxes and have a faith that transcends these limitations? Only one way: our faith must be tested. Here is an important principle that is so vital in the practice of praise. Without testing, faith can never expand beyond its present borders.

In this second sign, our Lord is testing the faith of this father. He believed in the presence of Jesus; could he believe in the absence of Jesus? Could he accept the radical notion that our Lord's healing power could reach out over twenty miles and touch the life of his son without the physical contact of Jesus being actually present?

Tests Are Never Easy

To appreciate how hard this test was, put yourself in the shoes of this concerned father. It is the seventh hour, one o'clock in the afternoon. You have been walking for six solid hours. You are a person of some importance. The King James Version calls you a "nobleman." You have servants and social status. Jesus can tell by your attire that you are a person of high rank. If your important position means nothing to the

Master, surely the precarious position of your son, hanging in the balance between life and death, will touch his heart. You come with high hopes and He gives you a rather sharp rebuke. "Unless you people see signs and wonders, you will never believe."

Although this is not directed to you personally, you are included in "you people." You don't deny the truth of it. Jesus' growing reputation as a wonder worker is partially responsible for you exerting the effort that you have made. Rather than becoming defensive,

> "Go your way,"
> He says, "with
> nothing but my
> Word to guide
> you, nothing but
> my promise to
> comfort you."

you humbly accept the rebuke and press your claim with even greater urgency: "Sir, come down before my child dies." Jesus seems to brush you off with a word, "You may go, your son will live."

Let me put it in modern terms. You drive clear across town in the worst traffic you have ever experienced to see a famous specialist. You barge right into the doctor's office and insist on seeing him. While he is examining another patient, you say, "Doctor, my son is dying. You must come now."

Without looking up, the doctor says, "Don't worry about a thing, your son will do fine." No examination, no diagnosis, no prescription, no referral, nothing. How would you feel? The fact of the matter is, our Lord often tests us in similar ways. "Go your way," He says, "with nothing but my Word to guide you, nothing but my promise to comfort you. I'm not going with you, at least, not in any physical sense. You must go it alone with only my Word as a lamp to your feet and a light to your path" (see Ps. 119:105). It's that kind of test that enables our faith to break out of whatever constriction has contained it. I say again: without testing, faith cannot transcend and a happy heart cannot progress to the next level.

Do the Great Ones Ever Doubt?

John the Baptist was a great man of faith. He believed Jesus was the promised Messiah when few, if any, others could believe it. Did his faith waver? God gave his faith a severe test. He was imprisoned. While shut into a cell, he began to seriously doubt. He instructed some of his followers to go to Jesus with this question. "Are you the one who was to come, or should we expect someone else" (Matt. 11:3)? Jesus didn't give a "yes" or "no" answer. He said:

> Go back and report to John what you hear and see: The blind receive sight, the lame walk, those who have leprosy are cured, the deaf hear, the dead are raised, and the good news is preached to the poor. (Matt. 11:4–5)

Was it possible for a great prophet like John to waver in his faith? You bet! What of those who have been incarcerated by illness, shut in by adversity, imprisoned by pain? Is it possible for them to doubt and nearly lose their faith? You bet! It's a risk God is willing to take. He knows there is no other way than the way of testing for us to experience an abounding faith that breaks through barriers and brings us to the next level of joy.

Much to the credit of this anonymous father, John 4:50 tells us, "The man took Jesus at his word and departed." He was not offended by what might have been regarded as a brush-off. There was something about that tone of voice, those eyes that mirrored the love of God and that face that radiated the conviction of reality. He simply took Jesus at His word and acted on it, and what a difference it made.

> The father simply took Jesus at His word and acted on it, and what a difference it made.

40

In this second sign we see a double miracle working. At the seventh hour when Jesus said, "Your son will live," twenty miles away, the fever broke. The boy didn't just take a turn for the better as the father would later learn when he asked about the time his son began to get better. The servants reported it was not gradual mending; it was a marvelous restoration to health. Verse fifty-two says, "The fever left him." One would expect a gradual process of convalescence to follow the breaking of such life-threatening fever. The perfection of the cure is what made this such a convincing demonstration of miraculous power. But the greater miracle is what happened to the father as he latched on to the word of Christ and made it his only ground of hope.

It's the Word of a Gentleman, so That Settles It

He had come with hurried pace, not stopping to engage in small talk along the way, but covering the ground as fast as his legs would carry him. In returning, he had peace in his heart and time on his hands. Had he hurried, he might have gotten back by sundown that same evening. But we find he did not arrive until the following day. There was no reason to hurry; he had his answer, "Your son will live." It's the word of a gentleman, so that settles it. Picture him coming to a lodging where he will spend the night. The innkeeper knows him and asks, "We hear your son is very sick, how is he?"

"Well, I haven't been home since early this morning, but I know everything is fine."

"How do you know?"

"Jesus of Nazareth told me so."

> The Bible is more than a history book or theological thesis on the nature of God; it is a love letter from home personally addressed to family.

If the reader will pardon a personal reference, when I think of the twenty miles between Capernaum and Cana, I remember the ten thousand miles between Vietnam and Fort Ord, California, where my wife and five children were living during our year of separation. There were times when I experienced a closeness to them that was nearer than physical intimacy. After all, in the spiritual realm, ten thousand miles isn't one inch farther than twenty. Christ is just as near to me as He is to my family. That means I am just as near to them as I am to Him. Therefore, the closer I draw to him the closer I get to them.

The most sacred moment of every day was mail call. I would open that letter and read the lines and between the lines. I could see the faces and hear the voices, and I found my family behind the barbed wire of a logistics base in Tuy Hoa. Distance meant nothing as we communed in spirit.

One day the thought occurred that the Bible is more than a history book or a theological thesis on the nature of God; it is a love letter from home personally addressed to family. If you are family, you don't have to worry about opening someone else's mail. It is individually addressed to you. You have every right to open it and feel the closeness of Him who is seated at the right hand of the Majesty on high.

How many light years is Jesus absent from us? It makes no difference. We see His face, we hear His voice as we read the lines and between the lines of the Bible, our love letter from God. Our faith pushes back the boundaries and expands into another dimension where time and space, if they exist at all, are only secondary. We experience the reality that the closer we are to our Savior, the closer we are to those who are dearest to us. What a miracle happens in our hearts when we rise above physical limitations, doctrinal constrictions, or traditional expectations and take Christ at His Word. Oh, that it might be said of us, as was said of this father, "The man took Jesus at his word and departed" (John 4:50). As he went, there was a spring in his step, a warmth in his heart, and a smile on his face. It didn't take much to get him laughing.

> The secret of a merry heart is taking God at His word and acting upon it.

Is the Bible Enough or Do We Need More?

Of all the principles of holy humor we will explore in this book, there is none more important than this: the secret of a merry heart is taking God at His word and acting upon it.

We see that clearly when we contrast the Samaritans of the town of Sychar with the nobleman in our Scripture. Before his faith was tested, it required "signs and wonders" to prop it up. The extraordinary evidence of the miraculous seemed essential for him to exercise faith. How different with the townspeople of Sychar. At first, they believed in Jesus because of the testimony of the woman. After having heard Him themselves, they could say, "We no longer believe just because of what you said; now we have heard for ourselves, and we know that this man really is the Savior of the world" (John 4:42). There is no indication that Jesus performed any miracles in Sychar. They believed in Him purely on the basis of our Lord's teaching, without wondrous works. No wonder our Lord said of them, "They are ripe for harvest." Whenever we can take God at His Word, we are ripe for an abundant harvest

> Whenever we take God at His Word, we are ripe for an abundant harvest of hilarity.

> True faith breaks through plateaus of reason and rationality and lifts us to new levels of joy.

of hilarity. Our faith has broken through to the next level. We have demonstrated in our own experience that the Bible is more than enough in all matters of faith and practice.

Another helpful contrast is that between the healing of the nobleman's son and the centurion's servant (Luke 7:1–10). I am indebted to William M. Taylor for his analysis.[10] The two accounts agree only in that the cures were wrought at a distance. In every other respect, they differ. The nobleman was connected with Herod's court and was most probably a Jew. The centurion was a Gentile officer in the Roman army. The nobleman came directly to Christ. The request of the centurion was presented by the elders of the Jews. One involved a son, the other a servant. In one the disease was a fever, in the other a form of paralysis. In one, Jesus was at Cana; in the other, at Capernaum. In the former, the faith of the applicant was so weak, he requested Christ to go to the place where the sick one was and heal him. In the latter, the faith was so strong that it could affirm; "Say the word, and my servant will be healed" (Luke 7:7).

In the one account, Jesus wouldn't go with the nobleman to test his weak faith that it might be strengthened. In the other, Jesus went to reward the strong faith and humility of the centurion. Being a man under orders, the centurion knew how authority works, up and down the chain of command. When he gave a verbal order, it was carried out by those under his authority. He applied that line of reasoning to Jesus. He was not worthy for our Lord to enter his house and lay hands upon his servant.

> As faith increases, our trust in the pure Word of God grows by leaps and bounds.

---

[10]   Taylor, 54–55.

It was not necessary. Just speak the word and it will be done. Jesus eulogized his faith. "I have not found such great faith even in Israel."

That's the kind of faith that breaks through plateaus of reason and rationality and lifts us to new levels of joy. That's the kind of faith that does not follow after signs and wonders. Rather, signs and wonders follow after it. And that's the kind of faith our Lord would inspire in the "royal official" and in us. The kind of faith that turns our frowns upside down so we can wear a happy smile.

In our story we have seen the nobleman grow in his faith. He began by believing the reputation of Jesus as a healer. Then he accepted by faith the word of Jesus concerning his son. Finally, when confirmation came, his faith rose to a new level which swept not only him, but his whole household, into the kingdom. Each level permitted him to be less dependent upon "signs and wonders." At the beginning he could only say, "Unless I see I cannot believe." You have heard, "Seeing is believing." No, seeing is only seeing, and sight deceives us in a thousand ways every day. Believing is seeing. Jesus had it right when he said, "Did I not tell you that if you believed, you would see the glory of God" (John 11:40)?

As the nobleman's faith increased, his reliance upon space and physical contact diminished in importance, and his trust in the pure word of God grew by leaps and bounds. That suggests a pattern for us in our spiritual growth. We want to reach that level where we can say with the psalmist; "He sent forth his word and healed them" (Ps. 107:20). As our capacity to trust the inspired words of Scripture increases, so will our inclination to "give thanks to the Lord for his unfailing love and his wonderful deeds for men" (Ps. 107:21). We will find ourselves more and

The words of Jesus saying, "Be of good cheer, I have overcome the world" is all we need to turn our grimaces into grins.

more in the house of God to "exalt him in the assembly of the people and praise him in the council of the elders" (Ps. 107:32).

Those of you who feel you are having a difficult transition from an immature faith that relies on outward manifestations to a mature faith that takes God at His Word, consider what a struggle the first-century believers had. Jesus sought to prepare His disciples in the upper room discourse recorded in John 13–17. They were accustomed to having Jesus with them: hearing His voice, feeling His touch, seeing Him in action. The day was coming when He would no longer walk with them but live in them by the power of the Holy Spirit. Before Pentecost He could only be in one place at one time, close to only a fortunate few. After Pentecost, He could indwell the lives of all who believed in Him.

When Mary Magdalene sought to grab Him by the feet in the garden tomb after the resurrection, she was trying to hold on to the way it was during the days of His flesh. But our Lord was ascending into a new realm of reality where His presence would be equally available to all. We live in that post-Pentecostal age where the emphasis is upon being *in* Christ and having Christ *in* us. The challenge is to live in the Spirit and walk in the Spirit, where time and distance, signs and wonders, and other external manifestations of miraculous power, are secondary to the voice of Christ that speaks to us in the Gospels. "Be of good cheer, I have overcome the world" (John 16:33 NKJV). This word is all we need to turn our grimaces into grins.

THREE

A New Level of Laughter

Cheerfulness That Hangs on to Hope When All Seems Hopeless

Some time later, Jesus went up to Jerusalem for one of the Jewish festivals. Now there is in Jerusalem near the Sheep Gate a pool, which in Aramaic is called Bethesda and which is surrounded by five covered colonnades. Here a great number of disabled people used to lie—the blind, the lame, the paralyzed. One who was there had been an invalid for thirty-eight years. When Jesus saw him lying there and learned that he had been in this condition for a long time, he asked him, "Do you want to get well?"

"Sir," the invalid replied, "I have no one to help me into the pool when the water is stirred. While I am trying to get in, someone else goes down ahead of me."

Then Jesus said to him, "Get up! Pick up your mat and walk." At once the man was cured; he picked up his mat and walked.

The day on which this took place was a Sabbath, and so the Jewish leaders said to the man who had been healed, "It is the Sabbath; the law forbids you to carry your mat."

But he replied, "The man who made me well said to me, 'Pick up your mat and walk.'"

So they asked him, "Who is this fellow who told you to pick it up and walk?"

The man who was healed had no idea who it was, for Jesus had slipped away into the crowd that was there.

Later Jesus found him at the temple and said to him, "See, you are well again. Stop sinning or something worse may happen to you." The man went away and told the Jewish leaders that it was Jesus who had made him well.

So, because Jesus was doing these things on the Sabbath, the Jewish leaders began to persecute him.

(John 5:1–16)

We have seen in the first two chapters that the transforming power of Christ is sufficient to turn the water of our daily routine, those colorless and tasteless areas that have lost their zest and vitality, into the wine of joy. Water is essential for life on this planet, but it is also a symbol for the boring sameness of meaningless repetition.

Even going to church, reading the Bible, and saying prayers can become thin and watery. We all go through dry and unproductive periods in our lives when it may be said, "They have no wine." By sheer willpower we may continue our religious devotions and duties, long after they settle into a rut of mechanical routine and are no longer fun. Good news: the power of Christ is more than adequate to meet this need and bring us spiritual renewal. How sweet the mirth when Jesus turns our water into wine.

The power of Christ is not only transforming, it is transcendent. It transcends time and place. It cannot be contained in the land of Israel of the first century. It reaches to the

> How sweet the mirth when Jesus turns our water into wine.

twentieth century and challenges the limitations of our faith, breaking into our personal
lives. It reaches across great distances of time
and space. Its power is not limited by nearness
or absence.

Our sense of humor prospers when we take Jesus at His Word.

Our Savior has risen and ascended into
the heavens. Not even the heaven of heavens
can contain Him. He says, "I go to prepare a
place for you" (John 14:2 NKJV). That place may be light years away.
It makes no difference. He lives in our hearts by faith, and His Word
reaches across the immensity of empty space. That transcendent power
is continually testing us so we can break the bonds of reliance on the five
senses and trust implicitly in the promises of God. Our joyful feelings
really begin to flourish when our faith no longer depends on the external
effects of signs and wonders, but derives its dynamic and direction from
the pure words of the Bible. How our sense of humor prospers when
we take Jesus at His Word.

The power of Christ, which is both transforming and transcendent,
is also at times, troubling. He loves us too much to leave us alone in
our complacency. Sometimes we settle into the comfort of mediocrity.
In the words of the prophet Amos, we are "at ease in Zion" (Amos 6:1
NKJV). He specializes not only in comforting the afflicted, but in
afflicting the comfortable. Sometimes He does both at the same time. The
consummate skill by which He performs this dual ministry is revealed in
our third sign, the healing of the impotent man at the pool of Bethesda.

A Man without Hope at a Healing Shrine

The pool of Bethesda was widely acclaimed in Jesus' day as a healing
shrine. Sick people would gather in the shade of the five porticos,
or porches, surrounding the pool, waiting for that magic moment

> The pool of Bethesda is a mirror in which we see reflected the depths of our own spiritual renewal.

when the waters were stirred, as if by some giant invisible hand. According to popular tradition, people believed an angel was sent from heaven to stir the water. We would find a more scientific explanation, such as a mild earthquake. But the first-century mind had no trouble believing it was a divine disturbance. The first person to enter the pool after this angelic agitation could be healed. Through the years, many wonderful things had happened that seemed to lend credence to this popular belief. We are not told whether or not Jesus subscribed to this local legend.

As Jesus walked by, scores of infirm people were lying in the shadows of the five porches. Only one would be healed. What of all those who were not? This is a question that plagues us today. For every person who experiences a healing, there are hundreds who do not though they may pray earnestly for it and believe sincerely it will come. In this chapter, as we focus on the one who was healed we see him as more than a miracle. We see this chronic sufferer as a sign pointing to what God would do for all of us. What Jesus did for this one infirm individual in a physical sense, he would do for us all in a spiritual sense. This pool of Bethesda is more than a geographical location; it is a mirror in which we see reflected the depths of our own spiritual renewal.

A Forgotten Man

Jesus would trouble the placid waters of our minds with this probing and penetrating question. It's a bit irritating, so be ready for it: "Do you want to get well?" What kind of a question is that, especially to a chronic sufferer who had been infirm for thirty-eight years? That's almost four decades, long enough for one whose days are filled with useful and creative tasks. But, for a man who is confined to bed, every hour must drag by like an endless night. We can imagine that when he first became ill, his loved ones and friends called on him, brought him flowers and tried to console him. Had he recovered, they would have congratulated him for his good fortune. Had he died, they would have mourned his passing. But he did neither. He just continued on year after year in his illness. Gradually their visits became less and less frequent. After many years, he was forgotten altogether.

That day, as he looked up into the kindest face he had ever seen, he could honestly say; "Sir, I have no one to help me." Who cannot feel the pain of this lonely person who was forgotten and forsaken in his long years of suffering? Our hearts go out to all who have been bedfast for long periods of time. More importantly, so does the heart of Christ. As Jesus looked down He knew the man "had been in this condition for a long time," so He did something about it.

The Lure of Illness as a Safe Refuge

Again, the first thing our Lord did was to disturb the placid surface of his mind with that troubling question, "Do you want to get well?" On the surface, it seems superfluous. Who wouldn't want to experience a miraculous healing and get well? Don't be too sure. For many different reasons, illness can be perceived as a safe refuge, a respectable retreat from the challenges of a competitive world. It's all too easy to retreat into illness to escape the pressures of a "dog-eat-dog" world of fierce competition. It's all too easy to latch onto

Those who doubt they would be loved for their own sake, find illness an effective tool to generate sympathy.

51

illness as a way of manipulating others. People, who doubt they would be loved for their own sake, find illness an effective tool to generate sympathy. They are afraid if they recover they will lose the attention they need.

Have you ever known someone who felt he had committed an unforgivable sin and accepted illness as "divine punishment" for his terrible transgression? His conscience was satisfied with the thought he was getting exactly what he deserved. We can only wonder if that had any part to play in the chronic condition of the paralytic man in this fifth chapter of John? In verse fourteen, Jesus says to him, "Stop sinning or something worse may happen to you." Is it possible that for thirty-eight years this paralytic had accepted his condition as divine retribution? Don't ever dismiss this agitating question as irrelevant. "Do you want to get well?" is always of first importance.

This question is even more basic and fundamental in confronting those with moral maladies. John 3:19 (NKJV) speaks of those who "loved darkness rather than light." They are content just the way they are. The life of wholeness and holiness has little attraction for them. They are satisfied to live without Christ and the gracious influence of the church. Until they really hunger and thirst for the wholeness that is in Christ, there is little hope for their spiritual healing.

And what of those who are psychologically paralyzed by fear and are afraid to run the risk of loving? They lie on beds of self-pity and false humility believing they could never walk the high road of faith with God. Jesus has a way of reaching through layers of false humility and disturbing our timid little souls with this question, "Do you really want to be healed?"

Some may accept illness as divine punishment for their transgressions.

"But Lord, I have never learned to walk on my own two feet, to stand for what I believe in, or say what I think. Leave me alone Lord. I'm comfortable to roll up in the fetal position and retreat into the safety of my own inadequacy."

A Modern Parallel

One day while visiting some church members in a convalescent hospital, one of the nurses said, "Pastor, see that lady over there? I've been working here for ten years and I don't believe she has ever had a visitor. Could you stop by her bed and just introduce yourself?" After several such bedside visits, one day Clara Howell opened her heart and told me her story. She blamed herself for a very messy divorce. Apparently, her only son took the side of his father. He never came to see her and returned all her letters unopened. She had been confined to bed for twenty years, and no one knew exactly why.

As she confessed her fault for this divorce that ripped her family apart she asked, "Do you think God could ever forgive me for such an awful mistake?"

Without thinking, I blurted out, "The bigger question in my mind is can you forgive yourself?"

"Pastor, if I could only do that I believe one day I could get out of this bed."

She started taking physical therapy with the idea of being able to use a wheelchair. Our senior-adult Sunday school class purchased one with her name on it. She started coming to that class and continued with physical therapy with the higher goal of learning to walk again. As we were finishing our new sanctuary, we built a ramp in her name. When we finally dedicated our new house of worship, she preferred the challenge of the front steps

> The question is not, "Can God forgive me?" but "Can you forgive yourself?"

> As she accepted the forgiveness of God, she found the courage to forgive herself.

to the gradual slope of the ramp. Leaning only on a cane, she negotiated the steps and walked down the center aisle of the sanctuary. It was an unforgettable moment. The air was electric with excitement as she sat on the front pew and participated in our service of dedication. Those who knew her story felt like singing, "When the Saints Go Marching In."

I think of Clara every time I consider this man who had lain for thirty-eight years by these healing waters of Bethesda, waiting for an angel to come and stir things up. Clara had been bedfast for twenty years. Her learning to walk was slow and miraculous, rather than instantaneous and miraculous. But her spiritual transformation was the most miraculous of all. As she accepted the forgiveness of God, in that inner healing she found the courage to forgive herself. It's just like Jesus to do something like this.

I had the privilege of reading a book of poems she had composed during her convalescence. I couldn't help noticing that as she progressed in her physical therapy, her poetry was salted with a delightful sense of humor that was lacking in her previous poems. Truly a merry heart is a good medicine.

Perhaps Clara Howell is the closest I will ever come to knowing a saint. When I think of her, I remember the story about a young child who was fascinated by the stained-glass windows of his grandma's church. He asked his grandmother who those people painted on the windows were. She replied: "They are saints."

When he returned home, he excitedly told his father, "I saw some saints in church."

His father asked, "What is a saint?"

The child replied, "Those are people the light shines through."

How true!

Jesus, who afflicts the comfortable, disturbed the calm surface of this chronic sufferer with hope. The question, "Do you want to get well?" suggests a hope that wellness is possible. Over the years his hope had flickered and gone out. He had first come to this healing pool full of positive expectations. But every time the water was strangely stirred and the rippling effect could be seen on the mirror-like surface, someone else beat him to the blessing. By the time he dragged himself to the water's edge, it was too late. After years of disappointment and frustration, he had given up and lost hope. By His question, Jesus is seeking to revive what he had lost. It is always the Lord's plan to rekindle our hope.

> It is always the Lord's plan to rekindle our hope.

But notice, our Lord does not stop with confronting him with a question; He presents him with a program. How cruel it would have been to stop with the question. It would be like confronting a hungry, homeless person with, "Do you want to eat?" Then, when his face lights up with expectation, to turn your back and walk away. Something within us says, "Don't tantalize me and don't trouble me with hope unless you can produce."

Jesus can deliver!

The most hopeful insight in this passage of Scripture is this: we don't have to wait for something special like an angelic visitation. Jesus was not about to hang around that pool waiting for some angel to get in the mood to stir things up. As He said, "My Father is always at his work to this very day, and I, too, am working" (John 5:17). Jesus is working today! The King James Version speaks about "a certain season" in which healing was possible. Every moment of every day is open season for our

> Every moment of every day is open season for our Lord.

Lord. Therefore, it is never too early or too late to ask him to trouble the waters. No one can jump in ahead of you because you have your own private pool in the depths of your mind. He is the light at the end of our tunnel; He opens the future with possibilities, and something within us can rise to this blessed hope.

The stick he holds out to us is the question, "Do you really want to be a whole person?" The carrot at the end of the stick is the hope: if I really want to be, I can, by His divine enabling. Whenever my will is brought into harmony with His will, there is sufficient power to produce remarkable results.

The Three Planks in Our Platform of Holy Humor

Our Lord holds out to this man not only hope, but a three-fold program: rise, take, and walk. Think of this not only as a program for wellness and wholeness, think of it as the three planks in our platform of praise. As long as we are flat on our backs, all we can do is kick, and we always find things to kick against.

"Somebody always beats me to the blessing."

"I have no one to help me."

"Why aren't the waters troubled more often?"

"How come those angels are not on duty?"

"And how come the church is so unfriendly, the preacher so boring, and the choir so flat?"

"Every time I go they are having another financial drive. They're not interested in me; they only want my money!"

As Jesus said to Saul of Tarsus as he lay flat on his back on the Damascus Road, "It is hard for you to kick against the goads" (Acts 26:14). Put into modern English it might say, "Why

> When we transgress the principles of praise, we just make it harder for ourselves.

kick a cactus, especially when you are wearing sandals?" The Old Testament reminds us, "The way of the transgressor is hard" (Proverbs 13:15 KJV). When we transgress the principles of praise, we just make it harder for ourselves.

Often He challenges us in an area where we feel so inadequate and says, in effect, "Rise!"

Rise? Do you think I would have lain here for thirty-eight years if I could do that? Why torment and tantalize me with the impossible?

We can kick against the injustices of life, or rise by faith in response to His Word.

But that is always Jesus' program—to challenge us with the impossibility of being "born again," to love not only our friends but our enemies. He challenges us to rise out of our complaining into the contentment of the Lord, out of griping and grumbling into gratitude, out of murmuring and mumbling into "making music in your heart to the Lord" (Eph. 5:20). We can lay flat on our backs and kick against the injustices of life, or we can "rise" by faith in response to His Word and turn our frowns into smiles. If we fail to rise to the challenge of the impossible, we are just as impotent morally and spiritually as the man in our Scripture was physically. If we take the challenge, it is amazing what can happen as we act in obedience to His command.

Break clean with the old life; eliminate the temptation to slip back to your previous condition.

"Take up your bed." Don't imagine the poor man carrying on his back a four-poster bed with innerspring and mattress. Jesus wouldn't remove one burden only to lay upon us a heavier one. Jesus was referring to a mat, something like our present-day sleeping bag that could be rolled up and easily carried over the shoulder. In other words, don't leave your

> There are times when we need to burn our boats and bridges behind us and make no provision to go back to past comfort and security.

bedroll lying there all spread out—it will be too tempting to return. Make no provision to retreat to your place of infirmity. "But, what if the healing isn't permanent and my tired, old legs begin to buckle after a few steps. I will need something to crawl back to." No! Break clean with the old life; eliminate the temptation to slip back to your previous condition.

The famous faith chapter of the Bible, Hebrews eleven, gives us one of the secrets of Israel's deliverance. "If they had been thinking of the country they had left, they would have had opportunity to return. Instead, they were longing for a better country" (Heb. 11:15–16).

It is too easy to return to our old enticements when we fail to put the past forever behind us. Christ is calling us onward and upward to a better country of spiritual victory. Having passed through the waters of baptism, we have died to our previous manner of life. It is dead and buried. We have risen with Christ to walk in newness of life.

When the Roman army landed on foreign shores, the first thing they did after establishing a beachhead was to burn their boats. It was their way of saying, "We have come to conquer and there will be no retreat." There are times when we need to burn our boats and bridges behind us and make no provision to go back to past comfort and security.

The third plank in the platform of praise is "walk." How far did he walk? He walked all the way to the house of God. Jesus finds him in the temple in (v. 14). That's a good place for someone to be found who has just experienced a miracle. Notice, it is in the temple that he first learns the name of the person who touched his life with glory.

Can a person receive a miracle from Christ and not even know from whom he has received it? Well, this man did. All over the world, the life-giving Spirit of Christ is raising people up to newness of life, and many are responding. How wonderful it is when they walk to church and get introduced to the One who is responsible and get some scriptural teaching

> Jesus cares enough not to leave us alone in our comfort.

that gives theological shape and meaning to what has happened to them. Throughout the world, people who have no contact with the church are being touched by the grace of God. Many of these people don't even realize who it is that touched them, why, or to what purpose. They need a body of believers to help them find biblical handles to get a hold of their experience and give it theological definitions that can lead them on to the next level of abounding joy.

In my view, there is nothing finer than to hear a gospel choir singing the words of the old spiritual, "Wade in the water, wade in the water, children, wade in the water, God's gonna trouble the water."

Something within responds, "Amen, Lord, do it again; trouble the waters of our complacency." That's the kind of trouble we all need from time to time because things tend to settle to the bottom and lie dormant. We need the pool of human experience stirred by the invisible "finger" of God and a happy heart to stir them up.

The wise men's report about Jesus, that "tiny troublemaker" of Bethlehem, troubled King Herod and all of Jerusalem. He grew up to become a man-sized troublemaker, who cares enough not to leave us alone in our comfort.

Stir us with hope, Lord. Present us with a plan and program, which, when infused with your power, can lead us to wellness and wholeness and cause us to break out on the next plateau of praise.

> God's stirring in our lives can cause gifts that have long lain dormant to spring into action and ignite fires of a fun-filled existence.

If I may change the analogy from a pool to a frying pan, some of us may have what might be described as a "sunny-side-up" theology. There is a clear distinction between the white and the yolk. We have the Bible all figured out and pigeonholed into various categories. We have boxed God into our doctrinal system. We can wear a happy face and have a sunny disposition because we are the good guys.

Perhaps others have an "over-easy" theology. They have turned their lives over to God, and now they can take it easy and rest on their laurels. May God put in the spatula of His love before we get too "hard," and turn our theology into scrambled eggs, a mixture that can be much more creative than the old arrangement. Such a stirring can cause gifts that have long lain dormant to spring into action and ignite fires of a fun-filled existence.

Too many of us have capitulated to the cult of comfort. So many of our high-profile, user- friendly mega-churches have chosen comfort as their strategy for reaching the unreached. The data seem to indicate the unchurched will not return to a house of worship if they feel threatened or ill at ease. If you want them to come back, they must have a good experience, which means, they want to sit back and relax and know the spotlight of attention will never fall on them. This is somewhat overstated, but you get the point. First-time visitors have to feel comfortable, or they will never become return visitors to that particular congregation. Whatever works in numerical church growth is one thing, but, as far as living in the spirit of holy humor is concerned, the sooner we get beyond this comfort mentality the better. The third level of laughter is not found on couches of comfort. It is more likely to be experienced on the horns of a dilemma or on a cross.

Why did it take thirty-eight years for the healing of the man at the pool of Bethesda? What about all the other sick people who were waiting in the shade of those five porches? We don't have all the answers. As we wrestle with the mysteries of good and evil, the suffering of the innocent, and the problem of pain, we are in the best possible position to practice the kind of praise that is precious in the sight of God. As we leave our flowery beds of ease and run the risk of walking on unproven legs, responding to challenges that are above and beyond our resources, we begin to get a taste of what a real sense of humor is all about.

> As we leave our flowery beds of ease and walk on unproven legs, we begin to get a taste of what a real sense of humor is all about.

One of the most thrilling sights for the football fan is the forward pass. When the quarterback throws it on the right trajectory, the receiver is able to run under it without breaking stride, stretch out to his full capacity and catch the ball on his fingertips. It is a thing of beauty when done rightly.

Something infinitely more beautiful is our God passing to us His vision for our lives. Habakkuk 2:2–3 (NKJV) catches a glimpse of it: "Write the vision and make it plain on tablets, that he may run who reads it . . . Though it tarries, wait for it; because it will surely come, it will not tarry."

This, to me, is the picture of one reaching out to full stride to catch the vision and running with it to score points for the kingdom of God. Professional athletes push themselves in their training programs to compete for fame and fortune. Jesus stretched himself on a cross to close the gap between a holy God and sinful man. The Bible says he did it "for the joy that was set before him" (Heb. 12:2 NKJV). Can we not trouble ourselves to close the gap between where we are and where we would like to be by the grace of God?

Humor may be just the lubricant we need to stretch out to our full stride. I can still hear my high-school track coach say, "Men, just go out there and have fun!"

FOUR

The Endless Resources of Laughter

A Smiling Thankfulness That Multiplies Our Meagerness

Some time after this, Jesus crossed to the far shore of the Sea of Galilee (that is, the Sea of Tiberias), and a great crowd of people followed him because they saw the signs he had performed by healing the sick. Then Jesus went up on a mountainside and sat down with his disciples. The Jewish Passover Festival was near.

When Jesus looked up and saw a great crowd coming toward him, he said to Philip, "Where shall we buy bread for these people to eat?" He asked this only to test him, for he already had in mind what he was going to do.

Philip answered him, "It would take more than half a year's wages to buy enough bread for each one to have a bite!"

Another of his disciples, Andrew, Simon Peter's brother, spoke up, "Here is a boy with five small barley loaves and two small fish, but how far will they go among so many?"

Jesus said, "Have the people sit down." There was plenty of grass in that place, and they sat down (about five thousand men were there). Jesus then took the loaves, gave thanks, and distributed to those who were seated as much as they wanted. He did the same with the fish.

When they had all had enough to eat, he said to his disciples, "Gather the pieces that are left over. Let nothing be wasted." So they gathered them and filled twelve baskets with the pieces of the five barley loaves left over by those who had eaten.

After the people saw the sign Jesus performed, they began to say, "Surely this is the Prophet who is to come into the world." (John 6:1–14)

So far in our studies, we have seen that the power of our risen Savior is transforming. The water of purification can be turned into the wine of joy. Those "six stone water jars, the kind used by the Jews for ceremonial washing" (John 2:6), present a vivid picture of man's attempt to cleanse his conscience through the rituals of religious tradition. As the miracle implies, something stronger than water is needed. The blood of atonement, symbolized by the wine, is sufficient not only to cleanse our conscience, but also to transform us into God's image. Don't stop with moral reformation; go all the way to the cross and the spiritual transformation of a new birth. The miraculous power of Christ is sufficient for such a miracle. Then you can begin on the first level of joy

This transforming power is also transcendent. Time and distance, as we saw in the second sign, present no problem. Therefore, the historical Jesus who died for us nearly two thousand years ago becomes the Christ of experience who lives in us today, by the power of the Holy Spirit. This local rabbi, limited

> Don't stop with moral reformation; go all the way to the cross and the spiritual transformation of a new birth.

to the tiny country of Israel, who could only be in one place at one time, has become the "life-giving spirit" (1 Cor. 15:45), everywhere present at the same time in His fullness. Just to trust in His Word is to establish a living contact with Him that reaches beyond the stars and transcends space and the need for physical nearness. As we become less dependent on the external manifestations, like signs and wonders, and more dependent on the words of Scripture, we find ourselves breaking through to the second level of laughter.

> As we become more dependent on the words of Scripture, we find ourselves breaking through to the second level of laughter.

As we saw in the third sign, that which is transforming and transcendent is, at times, troubling. There are moments when we might like to become comfortable in our mediocrity, when we might like to take refuge in some limitation or rest on our laurels after a successful but tiring period in our lives. We can count on the power of the Savior to stir up the water, to agitate us with some probing question, or to prod us with some impossible challenge. It's all a part of the praise program He designs for His children.

The Trust Factor

As we come to the fourth sign, the feeding of the multitude, we discover that His power is also trying. "He asked this only to test him, for he already had in mind what he was going to do" (John 6:6). He uses His power to test us in the areas of our weakness, so we might receive strength. Many of us are weak in the area of trust. Certainly, the trust factor of the disciples left something to be desired. Their admiration for Jesus knew no bounds. Who could fail to admire Him in His tireless

Could they trust Jesus and be assured He was in control, even when it seemed otherwise?

ministry to the masses of needy people? Jesus was their hero who gave himself unselfishly to all who needed His healing touch and clear insights. There was no lack of respect. The question was, could they trust Him and be assured He was in control even when it seemed otherwise?

Matthew's account of the feeding of the five thousand connects it with the murder of John the Baptist. "When Jesus heard what had happened, he withdrew by boat privately to a solitary place" (Matt. 14:13). That's a good time to "come apart" (as the King James Version translates it) before you fall apart at the seams. When tragedy strikes and one is plunged into the depths of grief, that's the time to follow the example of Jesus and seek the solitude of quiet and rest.

Mark and Luke also associate it with the return of the twelve from their preaching and healing mission to the surrounding areas. "When the apostles returned, they reported to Jesus what they had done. Then he took them with him, and they withdrew by themselves" (Luke 9:10). They were anxious to report back to Jesus and share excitedly the details of their mission and how they had effectively ministered in His name. That also is an ideal time to take a vacation. To get away after a season of effective and fruitful service and keep everything in proper perspective, lest one be carried away with one's own success story. Lest they take themselves too seriously, they needed

Lest they take themselves too seriously, the disciples needed a time to humble themselves by laughing at the humor that happened along the way.

a time to humble themselves by laughing at the humor that happened along the way.

I have always been amused by the fact that humor and humility are derived from the same root, *humus* meaning "of the earth." Yes, there is something about a good laugh that can bring us back down to earth and remind us we are dust.

"Is it true, Daddy, that we are made of dust," the young lad asked his father, excitedly.

"True," his father replied: "The Bible says we are dust and to dust we shall return."

> How would you feel if your vacation was interrupted by the needs of a demanding multitude?

"Well, come quick Daddy, there's someone in my room, under my bed, and he's either coming or going!"

The timing was perfect. Jesus was at the height of His popularity and the crowds were getting larger and larger. Mark informs us that, "So many people were coming and going that they did not even have a chance to eat" (Mark 6:31). No doubt, Jesus and His disciples looked forward to a little respite where they could withdraw and retreat from their hectic schedule and talk things over privately. They couldn't wait to share both the sadness and the gladness.

But it was not to be. The crowds saw them get into the boat and head across to the other side of the lake. Hurrying by foot, the multitudes outdistanced the boat and were already there as a welcome committee when Jesus arrived on the other side.

> Jesus has the plan and the power to carry it out.

How would you feel if your vacation was interrupted by the needs of a demanding multitude? "Jesus touch me! Jesus heal my child!" Were there a hint of selfishness, a trace of mean-spiritedness in Jesus, here is the place it would have surfaced. But He rose

> If the trust factor is lacking, that will be the area where the trying power of Christ will test us.

to the challenge and "had compassion on them, because they were like sheep without a shepherd. So he began teaching them many things" (Mark 6:34). They were captivated by His smiling countenance. He was pure pleasure to listen to. Never a dull moment. I think I can hear laughter, lilting through the multitude like a fresh breeze.

He continued teaching and healing them throughout the day. As the shadows of the afternoon began to lengthen, the disciples became more and more concerned. Their admiration for the Master grew to new heights as He threw himself into the work of ministry.

But what about the practical necessity of feeding such a mob? What do we do when hunger sets in and they turn to us for physical sustenance? We could have a crowd of unhappy campers. Yet, he goes right on with ministry, as though this were not a problem. Imagine their consternation when he asks Philip, "Where shall we buy bread for these people to eat" (John 6:5)? *Dear Lord, we were hoping you had that all figured out. Now what will we do?* But He was testing them. He already knew what He would do. He had the plan and the power to carry it out. What a lesson for us!

I know few people who do not have immense respect and admiration for Jesus. The great majority have no problem praising Him as the greatest man who ever lived. The question for us, as it was with the disciples, is can we trust Him? Do we believe He is in control? Are we assured He is working everything out for God's glory and our good? Are we convinced He has the unlimited resources to accomplish the task? If the trust factor is lacking, that will be the area where the trying power of Christ will test us.

Trusting His Marvelous Multiplication

First, can we trust Him in His divine ability to multiply our meager resources so they go far beyond their own natural potential? Can you imagine providing a meal for 5,000 hungry men, plus a greater number of women and children who were not included in the count? The task would be staggering even for a professional catering company. Limited to a grocery list that included five loaves of bread and two small fish, Jesus did it with an effortless grace which still amazes us. Truly it was a miracle of multiplication that only God in His magnificence could perform.

> Can we trust in Christ's divine ability to multiply our meager resources so they go far beyond their own natural potential?

Consider the creative power of His marvelous multiplication; five loaves and two small fish, just enough for a growing boy's lunch. Yet, in the miracle-working hands of the Master it was enough to feed a multitude. It's not that each one got just a symbolic bite, like the paper-thin wafer and the tiny cup we serve at Communion. Each one received enough to be satisfied. Whatever amount was required to satisfy each person's need was available. Some of the adults needed more, the children required less; there was sufficient for all. When the miracle was completed, they ended up with more than when they started. They started with barely half a basket. They finished with twelve baskets, all filled to the brim with food and enough for the twelve grown men who had done the serving.

Can't you picture an apostle taking the plate of two fishes from the hands of Jesus and handing it to someone sitting on the grass. He turns back to get the plate of five morsels of bread. As he passes it, he notices the plate of fish is still moving through the seated multitude. People are

> So many of God's miracles of provision never call attention to themselves, but are signs pointing to the abundance of our Great Provider.

withdrawing from it as much as they need. He returns for another plate of fish and another plate of bread. The supply is undiminished. As fast as they pass it out it fills up to the brim. Imagine their faces lighting up with the humor of amazement and surprise at this miracle of multiplication. Serving this multitude was the height of enjoyment.

When did the multiplication process begin? When Jesus broke the bread? When He passed it to the disciples? As they distributed it to the people? As each person received it in his or her own hands? I don't know. Perhaps it occurred throughout the whole process of distribution. I think it happened so quietly, so unobtrusively, like leaven working in a lump of dough that people were not even aware that a miracle was occurring. It was only later, when the full impact dawned that people began to think, how did He do that? How could so little go so far? What kind of person is this Jesus?

So many of God's miracles of provision occur like that. They never call attention to themselves but are like signs pointing to the abundance of our Great Provider and the smiling countenance of the Comic Spirit of creation. They seem to happen very effortlessly as we go about passing on to others what God has provided for us. It is only afterwards that the full impact is felt.

John 6:11 informs us that Jesus first gave thanks before He began the distribution process. It is easy to be thankful after the miracle occurs. Jesus was completely grateful for whatever His Father had provided, even if it seemed hopelessly inadequate at the time. He might have taken his cue from Andrew, "How far will they go among so many" (John 6:9)? He might have looked out upon the hungry multitude, looked down on the meager supply and looked up and prayed; "Father, surely You can do better than this!" But He was entirely thankful for whatever His heavenly Father had provided before the miracle of multiplication had occurred.

> Our little always goes further after it is blessed with a laughing spirit of thanksgiving.

On that basis, I want to suggest that our little always goes further after it is blessed with a laughing spirit of thanksgiving. We get more bounce to the ounce, more bang for the buck, more go to the gallon when we find ourselves thankful for whatever we see God doing. I can't explain it; it is a miracle! But I know it happens every day in our lives as we trust God to supply. We can "serve the Lord with gladness and enter his courts with praise" (Ps. 100:2 KJV). Our grumpiness and grouchiness can be turned into a grin when gratitude enters in.

If you are having trouble making ends meet, let me suggest an attitude check. Check your attitude of gratitude along the lines of the latitude of love. It is no secret; those who are less than thankful require more of everything in life, and in the end, have less to show for it. On the other hand, there is nothing that stretches this world's goods more than a grateful heart.

> Our grumpiness and grouchiness can be turned into a grin when gratitude enters in.

Experiencing a surplus is always a lot easier when the gap is filled with songs of thanksgiving. When thanksgiving leads to thanks-living, those ends not only meet, they overlap. That shouldn't seem so strange. Our God invented the multiplication tables long before man discovered them.

Like Philip who was thinking small—just "for each one to have a bite" (John 6:7)—often we set our sights too low. We think in terms of bare necessities rather than supernatural surplus. We forget that God has promised to "meet all your needs according to his glorious riches in Christ Jesus" (Phil. 4:19). Those "glorious riches in Christ Jesus," not only know how to add but also to multiply.

In light of this miraculous sign, we can say God desires, out of His lavish abundance, to multiply us until we can say, "The Lord is my shepherd, I shall not be in want" (Ps. 23:1). God is not limited to our needs; He can satisfy our wants as well; especially when our wants are godly, inspired within us by the Holy Spirit.

Remember what He promised Abraham? "I will make my covenant between Me and you, and will multiply you exceedingly" (Gen. 17:2 NKJV). Are we not children of the covenant and spiritual descendants of Abraham through faith in the promised seed the Lord Jesus Christ? Abraham's God is our God; He wants to multiply us exceedingly until our baskets are full and overflowing.

Trusting His Management

Can we trust Jesus in His ability to organize the details of our lives, so we can perform at maximum efficiency? As we let this sign point us to the "scenic route," we may catch a glimpse of the majesty of Jesus' marvelous management. How wonderfully organized He is. It didn't seem to be so from the disciples' perspective. That's why they were so worried. No sooner had they beached their boat on the eastern shore of Lake Galilee than they were besieged by a multitude. So absorbed was Jesus in His work of teaching and healing, that it seemed to them that He had lost all track of time and place.

It is never the plan of Jesus to send people away. He has the resources and knows how to manage them to meet every emergency and contingency.

Jesus is so busy telling them about heaven, he has forgotten they have stomachs to fill. Finally, their only recommendation was, "Send the crowds away, so they can go to the villages and buy themselves some food" (Matt. 14:15). That's all they could suggest. Cut the people loose so all can fend for themselves. It is never the plan of Jesus to send people away. It is not necessary to dismiss anyone, for He has the resources and He knows how to manage them to meet every emergency and contingency.

He knew exactly what He was going to do and how He was going to do it. The Synoptic Gospels inform us that Jesus had everybody sit down. There is great wisdom in this. Sometimes hungry people can push and shove as they stampede for food. Sitting down was the way to solve that problem. Management principle number two: he had them seated in groups of fifty and one hundred. Breaking the multitude down into smaller sections made it much easier for the disciples to serve them. Everything went like clockwork, like a well-oiled machine. There was not a wasted motion as the bread was passed from Jesus to the disciples, to the groups, and finally to each person in the group. Only a superb administrator could orchestrate something like this. Jesus obviously has the gift of administration; He knows how to organize everything so it runs smoothly with the least amount of effort. Whenever things are not running as efficiently as we would like, we can do no better than put ourselves under new management. Anyone who can feed five thousand hungry men, plus women and children, with effortless ease, so there is not a wasted motion, deserves a try. You'll find he is a superb manager.

What a lesson for the church. If we are going to do a lot with a little, we must know exactly what our mission is and organize ourselves to do it. The less we have to work with, the more organized we must be. Some churches seem to say, "We don't believe in methods, in plans and programs, we are just depending upon the Holy Spirit to work." On the surface that sounds very spiritual. The fallacy is, the God who does everything "decently and in order" (1 Cor. 14:40 NKJV) delights to work through surrendered, Spirit-filled organization. If the church is going to serve the world more efficiently, it must plan its work and work its plans in the realization that God works through organization, not around it.

Trusting Him in the Minute Details of Life

> We can trust our Lord in the smallest details of life.

Our marvelous multiplier, who is also a masterful manager, is mindful of the minute. That is one of His most majestic traits, which shines through this fourth sign. We often speak of micromanagement as though it were a bad thing. As human beings it is so easy for us to lose the big picture and get bogged down in the "nut and bolts" of running a business. But our Lord is a superb micromanager. We can trust Him, not only with the big things, but in the smallest details of life.

The psalmist asks the question, "What is man that Thou art mindful of him" (Ps. 8:4 KJV). This speck of cosmic dust, how could God be mindful of him? This is true because the God of the galaxies is also the activator of the atom. He is concerned, not only for kings, but for crumbs. Listen to the words of Jesus recorded in John 6:12 (NKJV): "So when they were filled, He said to His disciples, 'Gather up the fragments that remain, so that nothing is lost.'"

The Savior of the solar system, who is lavish in His abundance, is also the mover of the molecule who is thrifty in His conservation.

> He gathers up the broken fragments of our lives, breathes new life into them, and reshapes them into a more Christ-like pattern.

> If we commit all to Him, nothing is lost. If we commit nothing to Christ, all is lost.

He desires every fragment to be conserved and preserved for future use. It is in His divine nature to gather up the broken fragments of our lives with great care, breathe new life into them, and reshape them into a more Christ-like pattern, so they can be recycled on a higher plane. The good news is, when we give our all to the Savior, nothing is lost because He gathers up every fragment and puts them together in a pattern that has eternal meaning and value. That's a thought that can turn a frown upside down.

Trusting Him to Keep What We Commit

The apostle Paul was absolutely convinced of this, and it kept him going and glowing for the Lord. "For I know whom I have believed and am persuaded that He is able to keep what I have committed to Him until that Day" (2 Tim. 1:12 NKJV). What a praise that Jesus is able to keep what we commit. If we commit all to Him, nothing is lost. If we commit much to Him, little is lost. If we commit little to Him, much is lost, and if we commit nothing to Him, all is lost.

I wonder if the anonymous boy in our Scripture was tempted to keep back part of his lunch. Why not save one of those barley cakes just in case? But he handed over his whole lunch to the Master. What was insufficient in his small hands was all sufficient in the miracle working hands of Jesus. This young child leads us to the conviction that we should never hesitate to surrender our all.

The aspect of the miracle that impresses us deeply is not just how thankful or how organized Jesus was. We rather expect that. What

> There's nothing so big in this vast universe that it's too hard for God.

> There is nothing so small in your life that it escapes His care and concern.

catches us by surprise is how dependent He was upon a child and that child's willingness to share. The great miracle worker, who can do so much with so little, needs a little to start with. For this He needed the help of a child.

Often in our ministries, we look right through children as if they don't exist. May this inspired phrase be seared into our conscience: "Here is a boy," and you dare not overlook him. Regardless of your chronological age, a creative child is hiding deep inside you. I want to speak to that creative child within us. There is nothing so big in this vast universe that it's too hard for God. Likewise, there is nothing so small in your life that it would escape His care and concern. Every crumb that falls from the master's table, He would carefully gather and recycle for His glory. My creative child leaps with joy to hear news like that.

All through His earthly ministry, Jesus emphasized little things: the lily of the field, rather than the field of lilies; the mustard seed of faith, and the tiny sparrow. He said, "Whoever can be trusted with very little can also be trusted with much" (Luke 16:10). Often, we are tempted to think: *If I had a million dollars, I would be generous with the church and other worthy causes.* That is the devil's delusion. If we are not being faithful with our dimes and dollars, we would not be any more faithful if they were multiplied into millions. So often we hide behind excuses: *If I only had more faith, if I only knew the Bible better, or had a more pleasant personality.* Jesus is always slipping behind our excuses and whispering into our third ear, the ear of conscience: *But what are you doing with the little bit of faith and ability you have?* We've got to start somewhere. Why not with five loaves and two fish? This sign points not to the stars or to the four corners of the earth, but to our own backyard and to the little things we may have overlooked.

Of the thirty or so miracle stories which are recorded in Matthew, Mark, Luke, and John, only this one is recorded in all four Gospels. It made such an impression on the disciples. The multitude was also overwhelmed. John 6:15 tells us they tried to compel him to become their king; if necessary, they would use force. The marvel of this miracle compelled them to believe, "Surely this is the Prophet who is to come into the world" (John 6:14). Only the Messiah Himself could perform so magnificently. We have every reason to trust Him, especially in His ability to take the crumbs, the broken fragments of our lives and recycle them for His glory.

> We have every reason to trust His ability to take the crumbs, the broken fragments of our lives, and recycle them for His glory.

Some years ago, an officer in the Salvation Army invited me to look at his "treasure." He took me down into the lower level of an adult rehabilitation center and showed me pallets that were piled high with bundled rags, torn and tattered. "Some call me the rag man," he said, with his face aglow with a broad smile. "I don't mind because we turn these rags over to the recycler, who turns them into designer clothes. We take that money and invest it in the lives of people who go out on our trucks and work in our repair shops and our thrift stores. With that support, we provide them an honorable way to recover their human dignity."

That's what I see Jesus doing in this fourth sign. He would conserve every torn and tattered piece of our lives and recycle it for His glory.

FIVE

Laughter That Lives Above Circumstances

A Power That Walks on Water

> Jesus, knowing that they intended to come and make him king by force, withdrew again to a mountain by himself. When evening came, his disciples went down to the lake, where they got into a boat and set off across the lake for Capernaum. By now it was dark, and Jesus had not yet joined them. A strong wind was blowing and the waters grew rough. When they had rowed about three or four miles, they saw Jesus approaching the boat, walking on the water; and they were frightened. But he said to them, "It is I; don't be afraid." Then they were willing to take him into the boat, and immediately the boat reached the shore where they were heading.
> (John 6:15–21)

We are making good progress. We are finding every reason to praise our Christ of miracles. Who could fail to bow in reverence before a

> In Christ we experience a tracking power that never loses sight of us.

transforming power that turns water into wine; a transcendent power that heals over great distances and that moves through the barriers of space and time as though they didn't exist; a troubling power that cures the most chronic of conditions and offers hope to the hopeless; a trying power that tests our trust and can multiply our inadequacy until it becomes a surplus that is more than sufficient to satisfy those who hunger.

In this fifth sign, our level of laughter can be lifted yet another notch by the realization that in Christ we experience a tracking power that never loses sight of us, that reaches us in the most chaotic of circumstances when the winds are "contrary" (Matt. 14:24 NKJV). No matter how fierce the winds or how foaming the waves of adversity, it tracks us with the beam of omniscience and never loses us in the fog of despair. Our modern-day global positioning system is very primitive compared with the sophistication of His all-knowing.

He Couldn't See, Yet He Saw

Mark's account brings this out with fascinating clarity. "He saw the disciples straining at the oars, because the wind was against them" (Mark 6:48). What a vivid scene. At the close of a long day of ministry, Jesus had provided food for a great multitude. The popularity of Jesus was at such fever-pitch excitement, the crowd would use force, if necessary, to pressure him into becoming their king. Perhaps His disciples were being unduly influenced by this groundswell of popular support. He "constrains" them to get into a boat and head for the other side of the lake while He dismisses the people. As the people disperse, we see Jesus going up into the hills to pray.

Get the picture: Jesus on the mount alone praying; the disciples in the middle of the lake frantically bailing, three and a half miles from the shore. There is no way His physical vision could penetrate the darkness and the storm. Yet He "saw" them toiling in rowing and tracked their every move. What a vivid picture of the reality of life as it is seen through the eyes of faith.

> He never loses sight of us. What a stimulus for making merry unto the King of kings.

Jesus has been exalted to the right hand of the Majesty on high, where He "always lives to intercede" for us (Heb. 7:25). He has entered a dimension of eternity that is far removed from our space-time continuum; there is no way He can see us, yet He knows every detail of our situation. From that mountaintop of prayer, He never loses sight of us. What a stimulus for making merry unto the King of kings.

Life is Like a Sea of Galilee

> Our Savior is conscious of our chaotic condition. No matter how severe the situation, God is cognizant of our predicament.

Normally, the weather is good and the surface of Lake Galilee is smooth as glass. There are those occasions, however, when the wind sweeps down from the surrounding hillsides, turning this placid body of water into a boiling caldron of whitecaps that can test the skills of the most seasoned fishermen. Life is like the Sea of Galilee. Much of the time it can be calm and peaceful. But there are those crises when we, like the disciples, can be caught in the midst of a tempest. Obviously, this fifth sign points beyond an historical event. It is more than a miracle; it is a parable that points to the most essential convictions of our Christian faith. It presents a panoramic picture of our personal lives in the symbolism of geographical details, which highlight how we experience God in this present world. We must not allow the velocity of the winds or the height of the waves to obliterate our spiritual perception that our blessed Savior is conscious of our chaotic condition. No matter how severe the situation, our God is cognizant of our predicament.

I Can Row if I Know He Knows

Talk about signs. One of the road signs that gets my goat every time is that triangular one that shows a rock falling from a mountain and the warning: "Beware of falling rocks." It might as well say, "Dodge flying bullets." How can one avoid falling rocks? After they have fallen, maybe one can maneuver around them. If that sign gets my goat, it only proves I have a goat to get.

Here's the way I turn this old goat into a lamb. I remind myself that Jesus said not even a sparrow can "fall to the ground apart from the will of your Father . . . you are worth more than many sparrows" (Matt. 10:29–30). He who knows about falling sparrows also knows about falling rocks, before they fall, while they are falling, and after they have fallen. He also knows the exact position of my car as I drive under those overhanging ledges. What else is important? If Jesus is fully conscious of my condition, what else matters? I can endure anything with a smile, if I know He knows.

Another conviction captured by this parabolic picture is that the One who is conscious of our condition, comes to us in our crisis. Perhaps He waits till the most crucial hour, but He comes in His own time. "About the fourth watch of the night he went out to them, walking on the lake" (Mark 6:48). Why the fourth watch? Why not the first, second, or third?

I've heard it said, "It is darkest just before the dawn." That's just the time God loves to intervene. Maybe it took that long for the disciples to row themselves into exhaustion and reach the point of giving up. They were trying valiantly in their own strength to carry out the order to go to the other side. But, for every foot they rowed forward, the wind drove them an equal distance backward. They were exhausting themselves and had nothing to show for it. Sound familiar? Perhaps they were on the verge of giving up, to turn the bow around and let the wind drive them back to where they started. They didn't like starting something they couldn't finish, but how could they fight against such a powerful force that was driving them in the opposite direction?

It was at such a crisis moment that Jesus appeared on the scene and made all the difference.

The Working of Two Laws

Another core conviction that comes through this miracle/parable is that the One who is conscious of our condition, who comes to us in our crisis, also challenges our conduct. He challenges us to conduct our lives so we learn to walk by faith.

The sight of Peter walking on water is a perfect illustration. When Peter stepped out of the boat and put feet to his faith, in those few square inches where the foot of faith touched down on the waters of life, Peter was miraculously supported. It was not that God suspended the law of gravity or changed the consistency of the water to support the weight of a human being. I don't believe any natural laws were violated to permit this miracle. Rather, while the law of gravity was working,

> The One who is conscious of our condition, who comes to us in our crisis, also challenges our conduct.

> **It's amazing what you can do when you walk by faith, keeping focused upon Jesus.**

another higher law that I shall identify as "the law of the Spirit of life" (Rom. 8:2) was at work. Through the working of this higher law, Peter was set free to do what seems to us, in our present state of knowledge, to be impossible.

We witness this kind of "miracle" every day when we see an airplane lift off from the runway. The law of gravity is still working, but a law of aerodynamics comes into play that offsets its effects. As we keep our eyes on Jesus and our faith focused in Him, we are supported where the soul of faith presses upon the realities of life. In that small area of direct contact, there are forces at work that go far beyond our current state of understanding.

The Danger of Distraction

Matthew's account informs us that Peter got distracted and took his eyes off the Lord. His first steps were so wonderful. Going out there to Jesus was the only thing in his mind. But then he began to feel the velocity of the wind and the spray from the rising whitecaps. Perhaps one wave rose so high it temporarily obstructed his view of the Lord. Maybe he turned around to his comrades who were in the boat where they belonged. *What am I doing out here in the middle of nowhere walking on water? I can't walk on water . . .* and blub, blub, blub, down he went. It's amazing what you can do when you walk by faith, keeping focused upon Jesus. What an unforgettable and highly instructive picture.

A Modern Example

There are contemporary examples of those who, like Peter, walk on water by keeping their eyes on the Lord. They might have chosen to stay in the boat. Their prayer might have been, "Lord, it is wet and windy out there, come to our boat and everything will be better." But they have some nagging vision pulling at their hearts. And so, they fling this bold challenge across the whitecaps. "Lord, if it's you . . . tell me to come to you on the water" (Matt. 14:28). When they hear the call, "Come," they respond in obedience and find themselves doing what cannot be done, because God supernaturally supports them as they keep their spiritual focus riveted upon Jesus.

> God supernaturally supports us as we keep our spiritual focus riveted upon Jesus.

During the last fifty years, I know of no more inspiring example than Mother Teresa of Calcutta, India.[11] She might well have been content to remain as a nun in the Loreto Convent at Entally, a suburb of Calcutta. She was very happy there for twenty years. She taught at St. Mary's school and became principal. God was blessing her work and she had a full life teaching and administrating the needs of the school. But an inner call was tugging at her to move out of the security of the convent and minister to the poorest of the poor on the streets and in the slums of Calcutta. She was granted permission.

At forty years of age she found herself stepping out on the "water." She had no grand plan all worked out in advance. She only believed God would support her where the soul of faith pressed down on the waters of human need. Without salary or support, armed with the four vows of poverty, chastity, obedience, and a free choice to give service to the poorest of the poor, she stepped out on faith. Who could have dreamed that in less than forty years, Mother Teresa's Missionaries of Charity would become:

---

[11] Navin Chawla, *Mother Teresa: The authorized biography* (Rockport, Massachusetts: Element Books, Inc., 1996).

The most flourishing religious order in Christendom; in modern corporate parlance, it would have grown into an intercontinental organization with a transnational membership, benefiting the largest constituency of the world's most abject poor. Without the assistance of either an army of executives or a battery of computers, telex and facsimile machines (but only a single telephone, which Mother Teresa was reluctant to install for fear of adding to her costs), the work took root in practically every city and town in India and in over 100 other countries besides."[12]

It is impossible to imagine what God may do as we step out in faith in obedience to His call. Perhaps, there is some reader who is ready for the adventure of a lifetime. You are ready to say, "Oh Lord, if it's really You, invite me to come to You on the water. Teach me to walk by faith, and even when I fail, be there to catch me and carry me back to the boat." Those adventurous souls might just hear the same voice Peter heard, saying, "Come."

Other Important Lessons

In addition to these core convictions, there are several other important lessons that are highlighted in this sign/miracle. For one, our Christ walks on the surface of the stormiest of circumstances. Adrian Rogers said, "When Jesus walked on that boiling sea, he was showing them that what they thought was going to be over their heads was already under his feet."[13]

> Jesus calms the sea of adverse circumstances and brings us safely to our destination.

---

[12] Ibid., 63.
[13] Rogers, 137.

When asked how we are, we hear ourselves reply: "Oh, pretty good under the circumstances." What are we doing *there?* Our Savior provides overcoming power to live *above* the circumstances. As Rogers puts it, "He is the Head of the church. How could anyone drown with his Head that far above water?"[14]

> He specializes in turning our alleys into valleys with light at both ends.

No wonder the disciples thought he was a ghost with His white garments billowing in the wind, skipping from wave to wave like an apparition gliding over the surface. Who wouldn't have been "terrified?"

He immediately calmed their fears, "It is I; don't be afraid." When they realized it was not a specter or some kind of disembodied spirit, "they were willing to take him into the boat, and immediately the boat reached the shore where they were heading" (John 6:21). What a difference it makes when we "take Him into the boat"—when we receive the real Jesus into the frail craft of our humanity. He calms the sea of adverse circumstances and brings us safely to our destination.

It is important for us to realize that our Lord has not promised us always smooth sailing. There are times when things can get rough and we are tempted to think that perhaps we are out of the will of God. Remember, it was Jesus' idea that His disciples get into the boat and head for the far shore. In fact, he "constrained" them to do it. Every agonizing stroke of the oars in the teeth of the storm was in His will. Even as their boat filled with water, they were in His will. They didn't have smooth sailing but, with His intervention, they had safe passage to the other side.

God has not promised us rose gardens or that we would be carried through life on flowery beds of ease. But with God in our lives, He has promised us a safe landing on the shore of eternity. We can trust the Lord

---

[14]   Ibid.

to lead us through the valley of the shadow of death and through the gorges of gloom and the seemingly blind alleys of this life. He specializes in turning our alleys into valleys with light at both ends. The light at the end of the tunnel; the "v" that changes an alley into a valley is the vision of Jesus walking on the water. Keep that always in focus as you see the storm clouds approaching.

We are inclined to interpret adverse circumstances as enemies that threaten to overwhelm us, rather than friends that are engineered by a loving heavenly Father to undergird us with the strength of perseverance. The first chapter of James gives us a whole new perspective. "Consider it pure joy, my brothers, whenever you face trials of many kinds, because you know that the testing of your faith develops perseverance" (James 1:2–3). Out in the middle of the storms of life can be "pure joy" when we realize the plan and purpose of God. God is not punishing us for our sins. He is rewarding us with His trust. He is confident we have reached a stage of maturity where we can handle such tests in a way that will result in the development of Christian character. The patience to persevere is worth the pain of whatever trial we must endure. Oh that we had the wisdom to see it for what it is—our friend Trouble, knocking at the door to lead us to the next level of levity. If we lack such wisdom, the verse five tells us to "ask God, who gives generously to all without finding fault, and it will be given to him."

Ask God specifically for the wisdom to see your circumstances, not as though God were finding fault with you, but as though God were finishing His work, "so that you may be mature and complete, not lacking anything" (James 1:4). If repentance means, "a changing of the mind," many of us need to repent so we can see our circumstances for what they really are and realize that the storm is the

> Realize the storm is the norm. It is normal for the believer to be distraught by adversity.

norm. "Dear friends, do not be surprised at the painful trial you are suffering, as though something strange were happening to you" (1 Peter 4:12). It is perfectly normal for the believer to be distraught by adversity. So, "take it with a grin, open up your heart and let the sunshine in."

> What is over your head and beyond your control is under His feet.

Ask the Holy Spirit to activate your imagination with this fifth sign. Ask Him to paint upon the canvas of your imagination in living colors this unforgettable scene: Jesus, with hair blowing, garments flowing and eyes glowing is coming down from the mountain of prayer to meet you in the midst of a tossing sea of adversity. He walks upon the whitecaps and skips over the troughs. What is over your head and beyond your control is under His feet. It is not a ghost out of the past but the ever- present Christ who is more real than the wind and the waves. Let your mind be filled with this scene and let it inspire joy unspeakable and full of glory.

SIX

Laughter that Knows What It Knows

A Power That Drives Away Darkness and Inspires a Smiling Countenance

As he went along, he saw a man blind from birth. His disciples asked him, "Rabbi, who sinned, this man or his parents, that he was born blind?"

"Neither this man nor his parents sinned," said Jesus, "but this happened so that the works of God might be displayed in him. As long as it is day, we must do the works of him who sent me. Night is coming, when no one can work. While I am in the world, I am the light of the world."

After saying this, he spit on the ground, made some mud with the saliva, and put it on the man's eyes. "Go," he told him, "wash in the Pool of Siloam" (this word means "Sent"). So the man went and washed, and came home seeing.

His neighbors and those who had formerly seen him begging asked, "Isn't this the same man who used to sit and beg?" Some claimed that he was.

Others said, "No, he only looks like him."

But he himself insisted, "I am the man."

"How then were your eyes opened?" they asked.

He replied, "The man they call Jesus made some mud and put it on my eyes. He told me to go to Siloam and wash. So I went and washed, and then I could see."

"Where is this man?" they asked him.

"I don't know," he said.

They brought to the Pharisees the man who had been blind. Now the day on which Jesus had made the mud and opened the man's eyes was a Sabbath. Therefore the Pharisees also asked him how he had received his sight. "He put mud on my eyes," the man replied, "and I washed, and now I see."

Some of the Pharisees said, "This man is not from God, for he does not keep the Sabbath."

But others asked, "How can a sinner perform such signs?" So they were divided.

Then they turned again to the blind man, "What have you to say about him? It was your eyes he opened."

The man replied, "He is a prophet."

They still did not believe that he had been blind and had received his sight until they sent for the man's parents. "Is this your son?" they asked. "Is this the one you say was born blind? How is it that now he can see?"

"We know he is our son," the parents answered, "and we know he was born blind. But how he can see now, or who opened his eyes, we don't know. Ask him. He is of age; he will speak for himself." His parents said this because they were afraid of the Jewish leaders, who already had decided that anyone who acknowledged that Jesus was the Messiah would be put out of the synagogue. That was why his parents said, "He is of age; ask him."

A second time they summoned the man who had been blind. "Give glory to God by telling the truth," they said. "We know this man is a sinner."

He replied, "Whether he is a sinner or not, I don't know. One thing I do know. I was blind but now I see!"
(John 9:1–25)

Limit Yourself to What You Know

In the previous chapter, we locked on to a tracking power that homes in on our situation, no matter how dark the night or how severe the storm. It beams down and follows us with the watchful eye of love. Who could fail to rejoice in such a power of omniscience that never tires in tracking our every move?

In this chapter we are confronted by a power that drives away darkness and inspires happiness in the hearts of those who experience it, like the testimony of the man born blind. There were many things he did not know regarding the theological controversies that swirled around Jesus and the Pharisees. "One thing I do know. I was blind but now I see" (John 9:25). He had miraculously gone from a world of darkness to a world of light and he knew it. For the first time, faces, colors, scenery were clear to him. It was all so wonderful. Of that he could bear witness.

As long as he limited himself to the realm of personal experience, his testimony was very powerful and persuasive. It's a good lesson for us as we seek to witness to the power of our conversion. Just stick to what you know and the changes you have experienced in your own life. Your religious opinions, your doctrinal speculations, your private viewpoints are not nearly as powerful as the simple, straightforward testimony of what you have experienced in your life:

- "Once I was lost, but now am found."
- "Once I was without hope, but now hope springs eternal in my heart."
- "Once I had nothing to smile about, now I can't help smiling."

> Doing the work of evangelism ceases to be drudgery and becomes delight when we humbly share how God is real to us.

When our witness is seasoned with a sanctified sense of humor and is centered on how we have experienced God at work in our lives, it adds a flavor which is very persuasive.

"Let your conversation be always full of grace, seasoned with salt, so that you may know how to answer everyone" (Col. 4:6). Doing the work of evangelism ceases to be drudgery and becomes a delight, when we humbly share how God is real to us.

First He Declares, Then He Demonstrates

It is clear that show and tell, or in this instance, tell and show, was one of our Lord's favorite methods of instruction. First He tells the truth: "I am the light of the world" (John 8:12). This is one of the eight, great "I am" statements recorded by John. This inspired declaration is repeated in chapter six, verse five. It is immediately followed by a dramatic demonstration, a parabolic illustration: the restoration of sight to one who was born blind. This again highlights the truth that every miracle is a parable and every parable a miracle.

"Since the world began it has been unheard of that anyone opened the eyes of one who was born blind." (John 9:32 NKJV). Check the Old and New Testament records and you will not find it. Perhaps, that is because we see not only with our eyes but our brains. Visual stimuli go from the eyes through the optic nerve to the brain. There these electronic impulses must be translated into visual pictures. The brain has a limited window of opportunity to learn to do this. If a person is born blind and passes this stage of development, it is highly improbable that he or she could learn to see even if the eyes were fixed. When Jesus healed this man's eyes He also reoriented his brain to be able to interpret these new sensations into visual images. Truly, this was a mighty miracle the like of which had never before been reported.

As remarkable as it was, it was more than a miracle. It was a sign intended to point to the One who is the light of the world. If he can restore physical vision in the most hopeless case, He can flood our souls with the light of truth.

> If Jesus can restore physical vision in a hope-less case, He can flood our souls with the light of truth.

Light Overcomes Night

All the darkness of the night cannot extinguish the light of one candle. When one opens the door of a lighted room, the darkness does not come into the room, but the light goes out into the night. Think about it. Darkness cannot overcome light but light can penetrate darkness. If our minds are dimmed by the shadow of doubt, when we open the door and let Christ in, our darkness cannot overcome His light but His light will dispel our darkness.

As we enter into this ninth chapter of John, let us allow the Light of the World to illuminate our minds regarding the problem of suffering. Why do good people, even innocent children, suffer? If He is truly what he claims to be, let Him demonstrate His validity by giving us insight into this problem that troubles so many thinking people who would like to believe.

The Danger of Going from a General Principle To a Specific Application

The blind man's condition was not the result of sin but an opportunity for God to work in a way never before seen.

As we can see from John 9:2, Jesus' disciples were also struggling with this question. "Rabbi, who sinned?" Their instinctive response to this specific situation was that someone had sinned because sin results in suffering. As a general principle, this is valid. Bible-based believers can't escape the conviction that sin indeed results in suffering. But, does my biblical insight have to result in dogmatic intolerance that may lead to bigotry? This need not happen unless we take the general principle—sin results in suffering—and universalize it. If sin results in suffering, perhaps all suffering is the result of sin; the greater the sin the more severe the suffering. Here, we are in danger of stepping over the line and allowing a valid principle to become prejudicial.

As we allow the Light of the World to shine on this specific case, we can see that sin was not the cause of this man's blindness. As verse three says, "Neither this man nor his parents sinned." This man's condition was not the result of sin but an opportunity for God to work in a way people had never before seen.

Scholars tell us the book of Job may well be the oldest literature in the Bible. It deals with the ancient problem of evil. How can bad things happen to good people? In one calamitous day, Job was reduced to abject poverty. He lost his children, his material assets; soon after, he lost his health. He was left with a wife whose only advice was, "Curse God and die."

Job had three friends who sat with him in silence for seven days. How comforting they were as silent partners in Job's calamity. But then, they each began to speak, revealing their doctrinal bias. They went beyond the general principle that sin results in suffering, to the absolute notion that all suffering is the result of sin. Furthermore, the greater the sin, the greater is the suffering. *Job, you are suffering greatly; therefore, you must have greatly sinned. Get it out in the open and everything will be better and perhaps God in His great mercy can forgive you.* The book goes on, chapter after chapter, with each of his friends suggesting that Job has done some heinous wrong and Job protesting his integrity. It would have ended in a stalemate, in what we now call gridlock, but God broke through and ended the debate by revealing His glory.

Judging Each Specific Case on its Own Merits

The Book of Job protects us from taking a general principle and turning it into a universal dogma. As we stand in the spotlight of the illumination that shines upon us from this ninth chapter of John, we can see each specific case in its own merits. We have heard people say, "AIDS is the wrath and judgment of God revealed through nature upon the sin of sexual promiscuity." To paraphrase the question in our text, "Who sinned that this person should have AIDS?" It is so easy for us, like the disciples, and like Job's friends, to go from a general principle to a universal, binding application. As we stand in the circle of the Light of Life, its ribbons of radiance would lead us to examine each specific case on its own merits and pray for discernment. "Lord, shine your light on this specific situation that I may see it through your eyes. It may be the result of sin, but then it may be for the glory of God."

> See each specific situation through God's eyes.

Not to Solve Problems but to Serve People

Although Jesus does not solve the problem of suffering in the philosophical or theological sense, He gives us a plan for dealing with it. It's a plan that is intended not so much to solve problems, but to serve people. In other words, the light of the Lord shines primarily on the person of the sufferer, not the problem of suffering. The man born blind was the one being left out of the conversation. The disciples were talking past him as though he were only an object lesson and a case for speculation. He was being used as a springboard to launch into a theological discussion of the causal relationship between sin and suffering.

Some Strange Notions

What about the strange notion of prenatal sin? Is it possible for a person to sin while still in the womb? What about the popular notion of reincarnation? Is it possible that this man sinned in a previous existence and the law of karma has caught up with him and he is paying the price by being born blind? That seems to be a possible implication. "Who sinned this man or . . .?" But how could this man have sinned if he were born blind except while in his mother's womb or perhaps in a previous lifetime? And what about the transmission of guilt from parents to children? Maybe his parents sinned, and he is being punished for what they did. Maybe they had a venereal disease and he is suffering the consequences of their acts of unfaithfulness. And what about the relative effects of heredity and environment upon our social problems? Our philosophically-trained minds can so easily suffer from the paralysis of analysis that we

Serving people in need was the center of Christ's ministry, not solving philosophical problems.

never get around to *doing* anything about the people involved. Not Jesus! Look what he says in verse four: "We must do the work of him who sent me." We are not to debate the debates, or talk the talk, or theorize the theories, but do the work. The center of Christ's ministry was not solving philosophical problems, but serving people in need.

Use the Resources at Hand

It would have been so easy for Jesus to go on for paragraphs in response to the disciples' question. But He doesn't. He gets right down on His knees, spits on the ground, makes mud packs, plasters them on sightless eyes and says; "Wash in the Pool of Siloam." In other words, He used the resources He had to help people. He didn't discuss how many angels can sit on the head of a pin. That's what we love most about Jesus. It was not the problem of suffering so much as the person of the sufferer who commanded His attention. It is very much as if He had said, "You and I have nothing to do with such questions as these. They belong to God. We are not responsible for their solution, and we need spend no time upon them. We have other and better work to do. Not the speculative, but the practical, demands our care."[15]

There is a lesson in this for all of us. Curious speculation is fatal to earnest activity. In the brief time we have to serve God, let us redeem every opportunity to labor in His cause.

A Darkness Worse than Physical Blindness

We cannot overestimate the restoration of physical vision. Being able to see the faces of his parents for the first time and the beauty of nature must have been overwhelming. As great as it was, it was surpassed by the

---

[15]   William M. Taylor, *The Miracles of our Saviour* (Garden City, New York: Doubleday, Doran & Co., Inc., 1928), 369.

LEARNING TO LAUGH AGAIN

> There is a light that is even greater than physical sight, as wonderful as that is.

spiritual light that illumined his soul. There is sight which is greater than physical vision and there is darkness that is greater than physical blindness. When he was first questioned by the Pharisees as to how his eyes were opened, he says, "The man they call Jesus . . ." He didn't know where He was or the full story of who He was; he only knew He was a man.

As we contemplate Jesus in the light he gives us, we do well to focus upon the matchless manhood of the Master. When they questioned him again, the formerly blind man had gotten some more light. In verse seventeen he says, "He is a prophet." His experience leads him to believe that only a man who speaks for God could have done what was done for him.

In verse thirty-five, a seeming stranger comes up to him and asks, "Do you believe in the Son of God?" He replies, "Who is he, sir?" the man asked. Tell me so that I may believe in him." When Jesus identifies himself the man replies, "Lord, I believe" and "he worshipped him." Now his soul is flooded with light and the light brings saving sight!

This is a light that is even greater than physical sight, as wonderful as that is. He had come to the saving faith that Jesus is the unique Son of God. Obviously, his spiritual vision went through three stages, each one higher than the last. There is a wonderful progression from "man" to "prophet" to "Son of God."

The better we know Jesus, the more deeply we are led into the mystery of His sinless humanity and glorious deity. This is so different from knowing others. "The trouble with human relationships is that often the better we know a person, the more we know his weaknesses and his failings, but the more we know Jesus, the greater the wonder becomes, and that will be true, not only in time, but also in eternity."[16]

A Sublime Purpose in Suffering

What about the purpose of suffering? Can pain ever have an ennobling purpose, or should we practice euthanasia and put people out of their misery? There is no easy answer. Like the man says in verse twenty-five, "One thing I do know. I was blind but now I see." We don't have all the answers but one thing we see very clearly.

> Suffering is intended as pruning, not punishment.

Much suffering is not intended as a punishment but as a pruning. Have you ever seen a vineyard after the vine-dresser has done his radical work? If you didn't know about vines, you might think an enemy had gotten into the field and butchered those plants down to their bleeding stumps. Surely, they will never recover. But the one who prunes knows how far back to cut each branch for maximum results, so the life of the vine will go into bigger and better grapes and not be dissipated in its network of branches.

We are so clever at feathering our own nests and building our own little kingdoms. God will sometimes cut us back, so more of the spiritual vitality of our faith will go into producing the fruit of the Spirit, which the Bible defines as: "love, joy, peace, patience," those nine-fold qualities of Christ-like character (Gal. 5:22–23). It takes a lot of light from one who is the Light of the World to see this sublime purpose in times of suffering.

---

[16]   William Barclay, *The Gospel of John*, vol. 2., rev. ed. (Philadelphia: The Westminster Press, 1975), 52.

We must never forget that it is the fruitful branch that is pruned so it will bear more fruit. Perhaps our times of suffering are tributes to our fruitfulness and are necessary for us to become even more fruitful.

Go Beyond the Miracle to the Glory of the Man

We must again go beyond the physical miracle to the spiritual truth it embodies. The title of Adrian Rogers' book, *Believe in Miracles but Trust in Jesus*, clarifies the issue. If we believe in the God of the Bible, we must believe in miracles. We serve a miracle-working God, as both the Old Testament and the New Testament amply illustrate. But we don't make miracles the object of our trust. Our total reliance is in the Miracle Worker Himself whose wonders manifest the glory of His person and how He works in our lives today. If we allow ourselves to become miracle-mongers chasing signs and wonders for their own sake, we will find that no amount of them will suffice. We will always need more, as the Gospel of John makes abundantly clear.

The more excellent way is to see ourselves reflected in the blind beggar. Like him, we were born blind. Our spiritual condition has reduced us to a state of poverty. No matter how affluent our finances, morally and spiritually we are bankrupt. We desperately need the one who is the Light of the World. We not only need His light; we need the miracle of sight so we can see all that God means to us. This requires more than instruction, allowing the light to shine, teaching people the plan of salvation and exposing them to biblical knowledge. It requires a miraculous, inner healing that is equivalent to being "born again." Only then can our eyes be opened to the light of God's truth. Only then will the wrinkles of worry be softened by the smiles of satisfaction.

> We don't make miracles the object of our trust. Our reliance is in the Miracle Worker himself.

SEVEN

The Seventh Sign

A Power That Raises the Dead

Now a man named Lazarus was sick. He was from Bethany, the village of Mary and her sister Martha. (This Mary, whose brother Lazarus now lay sick, was the same one who poured perfume on the Lord and wiped his feet with her hair.) So the sisters sent word to Jesus, "Lord, the one you love is sick."

When he heard this, Jesus said, "This sickness will not end in death. No, it is for God's glory so that God's Son may be glorified through it." Now Jesus loved Martha and her sister and Lazarus. So when he heard that Lazarus was sick, he stayed where he was two more days, and then he said to his disciples, "Let us go back to Judea."

"But Rabbi," they said, "a short while ago the Jews there tried to stone you, and yet you are going back?"

Jesus answered, "Are there not twelve hours of daylight? Anyone who walks in the daytime will not stumble, for they see by this world's light. It is when a person walks at night that they stumble, for they have no light."

After he had said this, he went on to tell them, "Our friend Lazarus has fallen asleep; but I am going there to wake him up."

His disciples replied, "Lord, if he sleeps, he will get better." Jesus had been speaking of his death, but his disciples thought he meant natural sleep.

So then he told them plainly, "Lazarus is dead, and for your sake I am glad I was not there, so that you may believe. But let us go to him."

Then Thomas (also known as Didymus) said to the rest of the disciples, "Let us also go, that we may die with him."

On his arrival, Jesus found that Lazarus had already been in the tomb for four days. Now Bethany was less than two miles from Jerusalem, and many Jews had come to Martha and Mary to comfort them in the loss of their brother. When Martha heard that Jesus was coming, she went out to meet him, but Mary stayed at home.

"Lord," Martha said to Jesus, "if you had been here, my brother would not have died. But I know that even now God will give you whatever you ask."

Jesus said to her, "Your brother will rise again."

Martha answered, "I know he will rise again in the resurrection at the last day."

Jesus said to her, "I am the resurrection and the life. The one who believes in me will live, even though they die; and whoever lives by believing in me will never die. Do you believe this?"

"Yes, Lord," she replied, "I believe that you are the Messiah, the Son of God, who is to come into the world."

After she had said this, she went back and called her sister Mary aside. "The Teacher is here," she said, "and is asking for you." When Mary heard this, she got up quickly and went to him. Now Jesus had not yet entered the village, but was still at the place where Martha had met him. When the Jews who had been with Mary in the house, comforting her, noticed how quickly she got up and went out, they followed her, supposing she was going to the tomb to mourn there.

When Mary reached the place where Jesus was and saw him, she fell at his feet and said, "Lord, if you had been here, my brother would not have died."

When Jesus saw her weeping, and the Jews who had come along with her also weeping, he was deeply moved in spirit and troubled. "Where have you laid him?" he asked.

"Come and see, Lord," they replied.

Jesus wept.

Then the Jews said, "See how he loved him!"

But some of them said, "Could not he who opened the eyes of the blind man have kept this man from dying?"

Jesus, once more deeply moved, came to the tomb. It was a cave with a stone laid across the entrance. "Take away the stone," he said.

"But, Lord," said Martha, the sister of the dead man, "by this time there is a bad odor, for he has been there four days."

Then Jesus said, "Did I not tell you that if you believe, you will see the glory of God?"

So they took away the stone. Then Jesus looked up and said, "Father, I thank you that you have heard me. I knew that you always hear me, but I said this for the benefit of the people standing here, that they may believe that you sent me."

When he had said this, Jesus called in a loud voice, "Lazarus, come out!" The dead man came out, his hands and feet wrapped with strips of linen, and a cloth around his face.

Jesus said to them, "Take off the grave clothes and let him go."
(John 11:1–44)

A Bird's-Eye View

We have been making good progress. We began our study where Jesus began His ministry of miracles with turning water into wine. This is a good place to begin because all of us reach those stages in our Christian walk where it can be said, "They have no wine." The wine

> There is enough power in the Christ of miracles to give us a new start in our lifestyle of holy humor.

of joy has failed. All that remains is the thin, watery routine of going through the motions of maintaining some semblance of a Christian lifestyle. The old zest has gone; everything has become colorless, tasteless and as insipid as water. Why isn't serving the Lord as much fun as it used to be?

Good news! There is enough power in the Christ of miracles to turn our water into wine and give us a new start in our lifestyle of holy humor. So, the first thing we have done is focus on the transforming power of Christ because it gives us hope. We can pull ourselves out of the bog of bitterness, the mire of murmuring and transcend anything that we have yet experienced in extolling the majesty of our God.

That brings us to the second sign, the healing of the nobleman's son. The transforming power of our Christ transcends all our limitations. It cuts through time and space as if they did not exist and brings the historical Jesus into our lives as the Christ of experience. The Word of our God is not limited by distance. It reaches us across the centuries of time and brings timelessness into our hearts. An obscure Jewish rabbi who lived almost two thousand years ago in the tiny country of Israel becomes more real to us than life itself. Truly, His power is transcendent.

That transcendent power often troubles us in our infirmities as we see in the healing of the lame man at the pool of Bethesda. It probes and prods us in our areas of weakness and challenges us to rise and walk. We can praise our matchless Savior that He loves us too much to leave us alone in our mediocrity.

> Jesus loves us too much to leave us alone in our mediocrity.

With the pressure of love, he pushes us to climb Jacob's ladder where the levels of laughter go higher and higher.

In the feeding of the five thousand, we saw Jesus trying and testing His disciples to temper their trust. They had great respect and admiration for Jesus, but could they trust Him to multiply their meagerness till it became sufficient for a multitude? We can praise our dear Savior, that He is never caught off guard; He is never surprised or overwhelmed by the needs of the multitudes. He always has a plan. He knows exactly what He is going to do and how He is going to do it. His resources are always sufficient for every need. What a recipe for rejoicing.

The miracle of walking on water demonstrated Jesus' ability to home in, tracking us with His love, following our every move. Who would want to escape His omniscience? As the psalmist so eloquently says:

> If I go up to the heavens, you are there; if I make my bed in the depths, you are there. If I rise on the wings of the dawn, if I settle on the far side of the sea, even there your hand will guide me . . . If I say, "Surely the darkness will hide me and the light become night around me," even the darkness will not be dark to you; the night will shine like the day, for darkness is as light to you."
> (Ps. 139:8–12)

It was pitch black, and the disciples were in the middle of the lake, at least four miles from where Jesus prayed on the mountain, yet He saw them toiling in rowing. Even when we lose sight of him, He never loses sight of us. What is beyond our view is always within His purview.

His is a power that drives away the darkness and inspires testimony in our hearts. Like the man born blind, we can testify to our experience. One thing we know, once we were blind and now we see. The Light of the World has given us the miracle of spiritual sight. With smiling faces, we can give testimony to that which we know we know. As we bear testimony to those matters of conscience where there is a measure of certainty, we find our holy humor rising to another level.

God's Clock is Never Fast or Slow

As we come to the seventh sign, we ascend to yet another plateau of pleasure. The power of our Christ is timely, never tardy. It is always in perfect time with divine providence. It didn't seem so to Martha and Mary. They both expressed their disappointment, "Lord, if You had been here, my brother would not have died." The implication is, "We sent for You, why didn't You come as soon as possible?" A simple note was hand-carried to Jesus: "Lord, the one you love is sick." The purpose was only to inform him of their brother Lazarus' condition. They trusted him to do the right thing at the right time. Still, they must have expected a rapid response. The fifth verse of chapter eleven affirms that "Jesus loved Martha and her sister and Lazarus." There was no question of the depth of His feeling for this family. Yet, as the sixth verse informs us, "When he heard that Lazarus was sick, he stayed where he was two more days."

In my mind I can picture Martha, the more active one, going to the window periodically, looking down the road for a familiar figure. Mary, who is more contemplative, is sitting in deep thought. *Surely He has received the message by now, why doesn't He come?* Death came, sorrow came, friends and neighbors came to mourn. But Jesus didn't even show up for the funeral. Love, apparently, does not always rush to the rescue and leap to the side of the beloved. Sometimes divine love waits to be gracious. And the seeming lack of response fills us with feelings of disappointment. We are soon to learn, along with Martha and Mary,

> A seeming lack of response may disappoint us, but sometimes divine love waits to be gracious.

that our disappointments are His appointments. And He keeps every appointment, in His time.

God's Glory and Man's Good

True love, exemplified by Jesus, is also tough love. It is sensitive to human need. Therefore, it is eager to meet those needs when they arise. It is, however, also sensitive to the glory of God. When there is a choice to make between the needs of man and the glory of God, the tough love of Jesus will opt for the glory of God every time. In the eleventh chapter of John, our Lord is waiting for a difficult situation to become impossible in order that God's glory might be magnified all the more. As the fourth verse puts it, "It is for God's glory so that God's Son may be glorified through it."

> The tough love of Jesus will opt for the glory of God every time over the needs of man.

By the time Jesus arrived on the scene, the body of Lazarus had been entombed four days. According to Jewish reckoning, the soul of the deceased hovered near the body for three days hoping for reunion. After three days when decay and decomposition began to set in, the soul left, never to return. After three days there was no hope of resuscitation. In other words, Jesus waited until all was hopeless in order that God might receive the greater glory.

> What glorifies God is good for man and his capacity to believe.

There is another reason that helps to explain this delay of love. In the words of verse fifteen, "and for your sake I am glad I was not there, so that you may believe." Ultimately, what glorifies God is good for man and his

> Even during the apparent absences of God, He is working for us in prayer.

capacity to believe. It is also good for our patience and humility. In our immaturity, we are inclined to pray, "God, I want what I want when I want it."

Tough love is inclined to answer, "Child, you will get what I've got when you get ready for it." What kind of spoiled brats would we be if we got what we want when we wanted it? Even as fallible human parents, we realize how unwise it would be to reward our children with instant gratification even if we could afford to do so. Sometimes the answer is "no." Sometimes the answer is "yes" in the immediate present. Sometimes the answer is "yes" in the future as we mature.

We are inclined to become impatient during periods of delay because we assume that nothing is happening. During those two days of agonizing delay, Jesus was working for Lazarus. He was winning the victory for him in prayer. This is brought out so beautifully in verse forty-one: "Father, I thank you that you have heard me."

When did the Father hear the Son? As he stood by the open tomb? By the tomb, Jesus is thanking the Father for the victory that had already been won during those strategic and crucial days of delay. Without those two days spent in prayer, Christ could not have done what He did when he arrived in Bethany. Even during the apparent absences of God, He is working for us in prayer. At the perfect time He will come, roll away the stone and call us forth out of doubt into a deeper faith.

From Paradise Back to Pain

The book of Ecclesiastes reminds us, "There is a time for everything, and a season for every activity under heaven: a time to be born and a time to die." Furthermore, God "has made everything beautiful in its time" (Eccl. 3:1–2, 11). Even death itself is beautiful when it is in God's time, when it is at the end of a life that has been lived for the glory of God. The death of Lazarus was blessed with such beauty.

I want to propose the radical notion that his resuscitation was less beautiful than his death. The eleventh chapter of John, one of the longest chapters in the Bible, has the shortest verse, "Jesus wept" (John 11:35). It is the shortest and, in some ways, the most profound. Why did Jesus weep? He knew he was going to call His dear friend back from the grave. I believe He wept because He was calling him back from Paradise to a world of sin, sickness, and death. He was not resurrected, only resuscitated, to grow older and experience death a second time.

> Jesus wept because he was calling his friend back from Paradise to a world of sin, sickness, and death.

Wasn't this cruel and unusual punishment? It was only permitted to corroborate the claim that Jesus is indeed "the resurrection and the life." It was allowed because it fit the Father's plan to glorify His Son. But it was no favor to Lazarus. It would have been better for him to remain where he was in the arms of God. Nevertheless, to bring us the realization that Jesus is the Lord of death, as well as life, it was incorporated into the plan of God. As Shafto says: "There is the reluctance to recall his friend even for a season to take up afresh the burden of mortality, but the faith of his disciples needed building up to resurrection-height, for all were thinking in the old, hopeless way concerning the death of the body"[17]

The question remains, what should we do when God seems to be unresponsive to our needs? We send prayer messages, like Mary and

---

[17] G. R. H. Shafto, *The Wonders of the Kingdom* (New York: George H. Doran Co, 1924), 172.

> We can use God's delays to demonstrate the purity and the constancy of our praise.

Martha. It may seem God is waiting in the wings, standing in the shadows of obscurity. Why doesn't He come to center stage and speak His words of truth? In moments like these we can sing out our love songs to Jesus and practice praise in its purest form. Purest because it reflects the clearest conviction that even the apparent absences of God are reasons to rejoice. God is God and the steadfastness of His love remains forever the same.

So often we seek the hand of God for His blessings. On this seventh level, we are seeking the face of God; we are praising God for the beauty of His countenance, not because of anything He has done but only for who He is. So often our heavenly Father waits till the last moment to intervene. We can use these delays to demonstrate the purity and the constancy of our praise. So, I say; "Rejoice in the Lord always. I will say it again: Rejoice" (Phil. 4:4).

The Capstone of our Lord's Power

It is apparent throughout this fourth Gospel that John is very selective in his choice of miracle stories. The number seven is not an arbitrary number. It symbolizes completeness. John saves the Lazarus story for seventh and last because it brings us to the capstone of our Lord's power over death. If He can conquer death, what is too difficult for Him?

> If Jesus can conquer death, what is too difficult for Him?

Adrian Rogers draws the vivid word picture of the four stretcher bearers who were carrying the paralyzed man to Jesus. The paralyzed man protests: "Surely my condition is too difficult for the Master, it is beyond cure." The man on one corner of the stretcher says: "Look at this right arm, it was paralyzed, and Jesus restored it to strength." Another says, "I was born blind, but Jesus restored my sight." The third says, "I was deaf and Jesus restored my hearing." The man on the stretcher replies, "That's just an arm, two eyes and ears. My whole body is paralyzed!" The man carrying the fourth corner says, "Let me introduce myself. My name is Lazarus." Thus ends the argument.[18] "The bottom line is: if Jesus can raise Lazarus from the dead, he can deal with any problem you and I will ever have."[19]

Be a Demonstrator

This seventh sign is the most dramatic demonstration in the entire Bible of what happens when love is linked to omnipotence. As Jesus wept, the people exclaimed, "See how he loved him!" Jesus didn't stop with the tears of love; he said, "Lazarus, come out!" By resurrection power, Lazarus came forth. Love without power is weak sentiment. It can do little good. On the other hand, power without love is terrifyingly destructive. It can do much harm. What happened at Bethany is a living demonstration of what happens when the two are linked together.

The challenge of this book is to allow the love and the power of Christ to join hands in demonstrating to the world that Christ is what he claimed to be. Truly, He is the "resurrection and the life." It is not enough to preach, "Christ is the answer." We must demonstrate it by living on a higher plane. It is not enough for the church to proclaim that all men are brothers. She must incarnate it in

> Love without power is weak sentiment. Power without love is terrifyingly destructive.

[18] Rogers, 174.
[19] Ibid., 173.

> By our lives we can show what can happen when love joins hands with power.

her corporate life by showing there is no north or south, Jew or Gentile, white or black, but all are one in the Risen One.

The world is waiting, not for a proof text or an argument, but a demonstration. When we provide it, the same thing will happen—many "put their faith in him—as happened in Bethany (John 11:45).

People who sell cars, vacuum cleaners, or whatever, most likely will have a demonstrator. The more effective the demonstration, the more sales they make. The finest selling point Christianity can have are disciples who are demonstrators. By their lives they show what can happen when love joins hands with power.

When Jesus announced to Martha that her brother would rise again, she replied with the standard orthodox Jewish answer. "I know he will rise again in the resurrection at the last day." Our Lord's response was to direct her attention from a doctrine to a person: "I am the resurrection and the life." In other words, the resurrection is not merely a doctrine, or a future event, it is the present reality of a personal relationship with Jesus. Our doctrines grow out of our personal experiences with the personhood of the Savior. Those of us who have been schooled in all the doctrines of the faith, need a daily reminder of this. Doctrine never saved anyone. Only a living person (Jesus Christ) can do that. Let us allow that realization to lift our hearts in holy hilarity.

"An old Eastern church tradition says that Lazarus laughed heartily for years after Jesus raised him from the dead. That is why Lazarus' home in Bethany, the Holy Land, is called 'The

> Doctrine never saved anyone. Only Jesus Christ can do that.

House of Laughter'"[20] (When I visited the town of Bethany on my last visit to the Holy Land, I couldn't help noticing a plaque on the door that was inscribed with the phrase: "House of Laughter.")

I can't help breaking into a big smile when I try to visualize Lazarus trying to walk out of the tomb bound head to foot in grave wrappings. The strips of cloth had been anointed with spices, which had congealed making a cocoon like a soft cast. It reminds me of one of those mummy movies. Lazarus is trying to talk in spite of the gag over his mouth. Jesus said, "Loose him, and let him go" (John 11:44 NKJV). Perhaps Lazarus was thinking: *Get me out of this; I haven't eaten in four days!* Don't you find that scene entertaining to the point of outright laughter?

In the days that followed people flocked to Bethany to hear Lazarus' eyewitness account. As he repeated it, I can hear him spice it up with holy hilarity. No wonder it earned the title, "House of Laughter." So many people were becoming believers as a result that the Jews were plotting to take the life of Lazarus.

Don't you find that funny? *So, they want me dead do they? Well, let them take their best shot, I've been there . . . done that. Let me tell you, those four days in Paradise can't compare to this valley of shadows!* Peals of laughter are resounding through the neighborhood.

---

[20]   Cal and Rose Samra, *Holy Humor, Inspirational Wit and Cartoons,* p. xvii17).

EIGHT

The Consummation of Laughter

A Power That Transforms Mortality into Immortality

Early on the first day of the week, while it was still dark, Mary Magdalene went to the tomb and saw that the stone had been removed from the entrance. So she came running to Simon Peter and the other disciple, the one Jesus loved, and said, "They have taken the Lord out of the tomb, and we don't know where they have put him!"

So Peter and the other disciple started for the tomb. Both were running, but the other disciple outran Peter and reached the tomb first. He bent over and looked in at the strips of linen lying there but did not go in. Then Simon Peter came along behind him and went straight into the tomb. He saw the strips of linen lying there, as well as the cloth that had been wrapped around Jesus' head. The cloth was still lying in its place, separate from the linen. Finally the other disciple, who had reached the tomb first, also went inside. He saw and believed. (They still did not understand from Scripture that Jesus had to rise from the dead.) Then the disciples went back to where they were staying.

Now Mary stood outside the tomb crying. As she wept, she bent over to look into the tomb and saw two angels in white, seated where Jesus' body had been, one at the head and the other at the foot.

They asked her, "Woman, why are you crying?"

"They have taken my Lord away," she said, "and I don't know where they have put him." At this, she turned around and saw Jesus standing there, but she did not realize that it was Jesus.

He asked her, "Woman, why are you crying? Who is it you are looking for?"

Thinking he was the gardener, she said, "Sir, if you have carried him away, tell me where you have put him, and I will get him."

Jesus said to her, "Mary."

She turned toward him and cried out in Aramaic, "Rabboni!" (which means "Teacher").

Jesus said, "Do not hold on to me, for I have not yet ascended to the Father. Go instead to my brothers and tell them, 'I am ascending to my Father and your Father, to my God and your God.'"

Mary Magdalene went to the disciples with the news: "I have seen the Lord!" And she told them that he had said these things to her. (John 20:1–18)

Not Just Reanimated but Totally Regenerated

Now that we have thoroughly studied the seven signs and the seven levels of holy humor they inspire, it is good for us to consider the sign of signs. It is the greatest miracle in human history. Jesus not only survived death, but His mortal body was thoroughly transformed and not just resuscitated. As Paul says: "The perishable must clothe itself with the imperishable, and the mortal with immortality" (1 Cor. 15:53). That's the great mystery which consummates our good cheer. The power of resurrection lifted the lifeless body of Jesus into a new dimension of life that was forever immune from sickness, aging, death, or decay. His resurrection is God's guarantee that those who believe in Him can look forward to the time when the Christ of the empty tomb "will transform our lowly bodies so that they will be like his glorious body" (Phil. 3:21). This living hope lifts our laughter to the highest level.

Like a Neon Sign

According to Acts 1:3, for the forty days between Easter Sunday and Ascension Thursday, our Lord appeared, disappeared, and reappeared to the disciples. Almost like a neon sign going on and off. That was the sign of supreme significance because it pointed with "many convincing proofs" to the reality of resurrection (Acts 1:3). The season of Lent, the forty days from Ash Wednesday to Easter Sunday, had not yet come into existence. When we turn to the biblical record, we find the emphasis is not upon the days leading up to Easter but upon the forty days after and the post-resurrection appearances that occurred during this period.

We count at least fourteen separate appearances recorded in the New Testament. On each occasion, the conviction was strengthened that the Lord was in their midst at all times whether He chose to manifest himself physically or not. At the end of that forty-day period, the disciples had no doubt that their Lord had successfully made the transition into an immortalized body. They could no longer fear death and would gladly die to carry this message to the whole world. The moral and spiritual transformation of these defeated, demoralized disciples into flaming evangelists who carried the Gospel to the four corners of the earth, giving their lives in martyrdom, is one of the most convincing proofs of the resurrection.

> The transformation of the defeated, demoralized disciples is one of the most convincing proofs of the resurrection.

Who Was the First?

By taking the four separate accounts of the Gospel and harmonizing them, that is, trying to arrange them in a sequential order, it would appear the very first to announce the resurrected Christ was Mary Magdalene, as recorded in the twentieth chapter of John. The accounting is also in Mark 16:9: "When Jesus rose early on the first day of the week, he appeared first to Mary Magdalene, out of whom he had driven seven demons." God chose angels to first announce the birth of Jesus. But He gave to Mary Magdalene the privilege of first announcing the resurrection.

I find that somewhat surprising. We might expect Jesus to appear first to Peter, their leader, or to John, who was most akin to him spiritually. I would have expected the Cosmic Christ, who now belonged to the galaxies, to head straight for the throne room of the universe and confer with the Father and Holy Spirit. Instead, he first appears to one broken woman who was shattered by grief. How like Jesus not to play favorites but to respond to needs. If you are not in the inner circle, not particularly close to Christ in terms of leadership in His kingdom, but you have a genuine need, you can expect our living Lord to respond to that before any other pressing concern. That's just the way He is.

The Highest Tribute

What a tribute to womanhood! A group of dedicated women were last at the cross and first at the tomb. Check the record. They were the last to leave the scene of the crucifixion and now they would be the first to arrive at the scene of the resurrection. While the city still slumbered in pre-dawn darkness, this godly group was on its way to a glorious new discovery. So far as we can tell from the inspired record, the very first word Jesus spoke after His glorious deliverance from death was, "Woman . . ." (John 20:15). I see that not only as a tribute to womanhood in general, but to Mary Magdalene in particular. Her tears are certainly an eloquent tribute of her love. It was out of her that Jesus cast seven devils.

If the number seven is used here symbolically as a number of completion, this may describe a person who was completely held captive by a lifestyle of sin. In the sinless purity of Jesus' manhood, she found a liberating love that set her free and restored the dignity of her womanhood. She loved Jesus for that with a depth of feeling which has, perhaps, never been excelled in the annals of church history.

Remember the occasion when our Lord was invited to a supper at the home of a leader

> In the sinless purity of Jesus' manhood, Mary Magdalene found a liberating love that set her free and restored the dignity of her womanhood.

among the Pharisees? As Jesus sat at table, an anonymous woman, perhaps Mary herself, entered and did a remarkable thing (Luke 7:36–50). She knelt at Jesus' feet, washed them with her tears and wiped them with her hair. The Pharisees were highly offended. They said something like this among themselves, "If this Jesus fellow were really a prophet, he would know the reputation of this unsavory character and forbid her from touching him."

That's the amazing thing; Jesus did know. His only comment to the host was, "Her many sins have been forgiven—for she loved much. But he who has been forgiven little loves little" (Luke 7:47). The forgiveness Mary had experienced from the sinless manhood of the Master, released a depth of love in her that changed her life and made possible the greatest gift that any human being, male or female, could ever receive: the privilege of being the very first to recognize the risen Christ and announce it to others.

A Tribute to Saviorhood

Mary's grief had become a disability blinding her eyes to spiritual reality.

We can view this first resurrection appearance not only as a tribute to womanhood in general, or to one woman in particular, we can see it as a tribute to Jesus Himself and His ability to take our exaggerated grief and turn it into praise. I say exaggerated grief because there is another side to Mary's sorrow. In part, it was an appropriate tribute to her love. But it had reached the point of intensity that it had become a disability blinding her eyes to spiritual reality. Jesus himself draws near. Somehow, through her vale of tears she cannot recognize Him. Verse fifteen informs us she thought "he was the gardener." Praise God, He was not the gardener as she was soon to discover. But in her grief-stricken mind she could only assume that some grave robbers had broken into the tomb and stolen the body.

That was not a very rational conclusion. The tomb was secured by a twenty-four-hour guard detail of soldiers. It would have taken a major miracle for anyone to sneak past those sentries and break into the tomb. But she was not thinking logically because grief had clouded her mind and incapacitated her rational powers. Those of us who have been traumatized by grief can testify this is what often happens.

Indisputable Evidence

How like Mary we are as we stand so helpless before the reality and the finality of death. Our tears are a fitting and altogether appropriate tribute to our love. But how easily they can become exaggerated to the degree we become blinded to the reality of life beyond. Jesus comes to us as He came to Mary. Grief often keeps us from recognizing Him and seeing all He wants us to see.

John "saw and believed" (John 20:8). What did John see that made him believe? He saw the grave clothes that had been wrapped around the body. Grave robbers wouldn't have taken time to unwrap the corpse. They would have carted it off like a sack of potatoes, wrappings and all. Had they unwrapped the body, they would have left the bindings behind, piled in a disorganized heap. But the linen strips were undisturbed, like a hollow cocoon. What had happened to the butterfly?

> Grief often keeps us from recognizing Him and seeing all He wants us to see.

According to Jewish burial custom, seventy-five pounds of various ointments were used in wrapping the body with linen strips (John 19:38–40). As the spices dried, they formed something like a soft cast, so one could immediately tell if they had been tampered with. There was only one logical conclusion to which a rational mind could come. The body had simply dematerialized and left everything behind and undisturbed. John saw this indisputable evidence and believed. But while looking into the tomb, Mary could not properly evaluate what she saw. It was this disabling aspect of her sorrow that Jesus would heal.

On a First-Name Basis

He does it by speaking her name. It couldn't be the gardener; the gardener wouldn't know her name. And the way He pronounced it; the feeling He put into it. No one could speak her name like that! She turned and there He was, big as Life. Isn't that a tribute to our Lord? He can save us from our doldrums of despair with just a word. The

The fact that Jesus knows us on a first-name basis is enough to turn our sorrow into song, our despair into delight.

fact that He knows us on a first-name basis is enough to turn our sorrow into song, our despair into delight.

In addition to speaking her name, I see Jesus doing something else that is a real tribute to His skill as a counselor. He gently leads her from the physical to the reality of the spiritual. The source of much of her grief was an overemphasis on the physical remains of Jesus. The body was all she had left. It had to be found so she could have something to mourn. When Jesus appeared to her in a physical form, she was overjoyed. She fell at His feet and clung to His ankles. Everything would be just as it was. He would walk with them as though nothing had happened.

But Jesus says, "Do not hold on to me," which is better translated, "Stop clinging to me." Mary is trying to cling to the past and the old relationship of flesh and blood. Jesus is trying to lead her into a new relationship. So, he says, "I am returning to my Father and your Father, my God and your God" (John 20:17). All that God was to Him, He would be to her and the rest of the disciples. He would no longer be just walking with them but living in them; no longer limited to a physical nearness of being in just one place at one time, but indwelling their minds and hearts as a life-giving Spirit in a far more intimate and permanent way than ever before.

All that God was to Him, He would be to her and the rest of the disciples.

The Fifth Dimension

In John 20:17 (NKJV) Jesus puts it this way: "I am ascending . . ." For the early believers, the ascension did not mean Jesus blasting off into some galaxy light years away. It did not mean distance and separation. It meant that He moved into another dimension where He would be closer and more available to them than ever before. He was ascending from a four-dimensional world of length, width, depth, and height into a five-dimensional world. That fifth dimension of omnipresence meant He would live in them and they would live in Him. He would be closer and more available than ever before and able to establish a dynamic new relationship with all believers everywhere for all time. That made all the difference in turning their sorrow into joy. Likewise, it makes all the difference to us as we develop our capacity for a merry heart.

What If?

Before we leave this chapter, I want us to summon all our courage and ask ourselves this question: What if Mary's first impression had been correct? What if this veiled figure blurred by her tears had really been the gardener? What if grave robbers had carted off the body to perpetrate a hoax? What consequences would that have for those of us reading these pages?

We cringe from entertaining such thoughts. Even the suggestion there could be alternate explanations for the empty tomb fill us with foreboding. I don't believe, however, we are fully prepared to experience the glorious realities of the positive until we have faced the grim possibilities of the negative. So, let us force ourselves to face the consequences of a religion without Easter.

Fortunately, we don't have to rely on our own understanding. Paul gives us a classical expression of "what if?" in 1 Corinthians 15:12–20. In those nine verses he uses the tiny, intimidating, two-letter word "if" seven times. He is asking, *What if it were all myth or a massive misunderstanding? What consequences would that have for our faith?*

The Consequences for Preaching

> Without the power of the resurrection validating every sermon, what could one preach that might make a difference in anyone's life?

Certainly, there would be grave consequences for preachers and their preaching. If Christ is not risen, we preachers would be found to be "misrepresenting God." We would be bearing false witness in proclaiming something that has no historical validity. In verse fourteen (NKJV), Paul says, "Then our preaching is empty," which means hollow, without real content, and devoid of any power to transform life.

Without the power of the resurrection validating every sermon, what could one preach that might make a difference in anyone's life? A clever orator might tickle our ears with some pious platitudes. No matter how pleasing to the ear, they would be empty of any real power to transform lives. One might deliver a dainty little discourse on "How to Win Friends and Influence People" or read a learned treatise on "The Psychology of Living a Well-Adjusted Life." One might present some moral maxim or ring the bell on some patriotic theme.

> The sum and substance, the heart and core of the Gospel message, is the resurrection.

There is a place for this kind of emphasis. But none of these things is equivalent to Gospel preaching. As we examine the examples

126

of preaching in the New Testament, in particular the book of Acts, we find the sum and substance, the heart and core of the message, is the resurrection. Remove that and there would be no message, only a hollow shell.

As a preacher, I have tried to imagine what things would be like without the dawn of Easter Sunday. In my mind's eye, all kinds of terrifying thoughts flash upon the screen of my imagination. The most conservative are these.

Had that figure standing next to Mary been the gardener, there would be no church in which to preach. Had Jesus remained in the tomb, the early Christian movement would have quickly and silently expired with Him. After the crucifixion, the disciples were broken, disappointed, disillusioned men. They were planning to return to their old occupation of fishing and try to forget they had ever met and believed in Jesus. What was it that transformed them from eleven frightened men who locked themselves in an upper room for fear that what happened to Jesus would happen to them into fearless evangelists? Only one thing can account for this revolutionary change.

Not only would I have no church, I would have no book from which to preach. Would the four Gospels have been written had Jesus' life ended in the failure of the cross? The greatest single contributor to the New Testament is the apostle Paul. In 1 Corinthians 15:8 he refers to his conversion as the last of the apostles to witness the glory of the risen Christ. Up until that appearing on the Damascus Road, Paul was persecuting Christians and trying with all his might to destroy the infant church. Had Christ not risen, Paul could not have been converted and would not have written the greatest portion of the New Testament.

Certainly, I would have no Lord's Day on which to preach. During the centuries of the Old Testament period, the people of God worshipped on the seventh and last day of the week in honor of the old creation. This was a long established and venerated custom that derived its authority

> The early Christians began meeting on Sunday in honor of the resurrection and the new creation it wrought in their lives.

from the Ten Commandments. The early Christians were, for the most part, Jewish. Yet they began to worship on the first day of the week. There is only one event that can account for such a drastic departure from tradition. The early Jewish Christians began meeting on Sunday in honor of the resurrection and the new creation it wrought in their lives.

As Sunday flows toward Saturday, in the Old Testament economy, believers were working for their Messiah and the salvation he would bring. In this age of grace, we are working from our Messiah and the salvation he has already brought. What better way to witness to this conviction than changing from the last to the first day of the week? Without that, I would have no Sunday on which to preach.

The Consequences for Believing

The consequences we are considering in this chapter not only affect preachers and their preaching, they affect all believers and our believing. "And if Christ has not been raised, your faith is futile; you are still in your sins" (1 Cor. 15:17).

Contrary to popular opinion, faith has no virtue, no merit or power in itself. It derives all its value from the object in which it is placed. People misunderstand this. Often, I hear this kind of friendly advice, "A person has to believe in something, so just find something in which to believe and believe it"—as though belief were the important thing in itself. Like water, faith cannot rise above its own level. Whether it is a sewer or a cleansing stream depends upon its source and what flows through it. If the object of your faith is a dead and buried Jesus, then your faith is just as impotent as the object in which it is placed. A dead faith cannot save anyone. A living faith demands a living Savior.

The Central Pillar

In the third and fourth verses of the fifteenth chapter of 1 Corinthians, Paul gives to us the three pillars that support the structure of our Christian faith. Notice, these are anchored firm and deep in the solid foundation of history: Christ died for our sins, He was buried and He was raised from the dead on the third day. The backbone of our faith is historical revelation, the redemptive deeds of Christ and not theoretical doctrines or religious speculations, which are subject to differing interpretations. Our faith is supported by historical facts. Of these three, the central pillar is the resurrection. If this were proven to be a myth with no historical validity, then this pillar would crumble and with it the whole structure of our Christian belief system. If the resurrection stands, our faith stands; if the resurrection falls, our faith falls. It's that simple and that basic.

> If the resurrection stands, our faith stands; if the resurrection falls, our faith falls.

Not a Way-Shower but the Way

People often wonder about this. Other great religious leaders lived and died, and their ideas and ideals lived on and eventually became a world religion of vast scope. Why couldn't this be true of Christ and Christianity, as it is true of Mohammed and Islam and Siddhartha Gautama and Buddhism?

What people fail to consider is that Christ made claims that were vastly different from any other religious leader. Mohammed claimed to show the way to God. He pointed to a religious program of doctrine and duty. He claimed, "If you will believe this and do that, you will find God." After he died, his doctrines and duties lived on and are still being practiced with great devotion.

Christ did not create something outside himself that would live on after He was dead. He pointed to himself as "the way and the truth and the life" (John 14:6). Jesus did not just show the way to God, He claimed to *be* that Way. In Christianity, the way to God is not a program or a precept, but a Person of infinite compassion.

Our Lord said, "I am the resurrection and the life . . . do you believe this?" (John 11:25–26). How can we believe it if He is not risen and alive forevermore? Either He is risen as He said or He is not. If so, He is all He claimed to be and more. If not, then He is an impostor who is worthy only of our contempt. There is no middle ground between these two alternatives. The resurrection is the deciding, determining factor.

The Consequences for Hoping

The question, "What if?" not only affects our preaching and believing but also our hoping. What kind of a hope can we have in this life for the forgiveness of sins? As our Scripture makes clear, without the resurrection we "are still in our sins."

I once conducted a funeral where members of the immediate family were practically leaning over the casket begging for forgiveness. My heart went out to them in their sorrow. But it was too late; there was no forgiveness coming from that casket. The loved one was dead. A dead Christ cannot forgive anyone anything.

Can you remember as a child playing a game in which you tried to hide from your shadow? It was an impossible game to win because our shadow dogs our footsteps, and there is no escaping it. But as the sun rises higher in the heavens, our shadow becomes shorter. It is finally obliterated by high noon. Likewise, there is no escaping the shadow of guilt without the rising of the Son of God. It is the light of His resurrection that drives away the shadow of shame and brings the assurance of forgiveness.

Not only our hope for forgiveness in this life, what about our hope for a life to come? As we read in 1 Corinthians 15:19: "If only for this life we have hope in Christ, we are

> The light of Christ's resurrection drives away the shadow of shame and brings assurance of forgiveness

to be pitied more than all men." Hope that is good only for this life is a miserable comforter. It carries us through our brief span of physical existence and leaves us high and dry at the grave, just when we most need something in which to hope.

> A hope that does not reach beyond time and into eternity is a pitiful and miserable comforter when we most need comfort.

The Christian hope is certainly not all "pie in the sky by and by." It is a practical and purifying hope that is real and relevant to this life. I have heard people make the statement: "Even if there were no heaven to gain or hell to shun, I would still want to be a Christian and live a Christian life because of the hope it has for this present world." Or, some may say, "Even if it could be proven that life ends at the grave, I would still want to be a Christian because of the motivation it provides in living a creative, useful life to the glory of God." In part, I agree with this. The motivational power we derive from a hope that calls us to be all

> Without the resurrection, the hope of life after death becomes faceless, an impersonal hope of diminished survival in an ethereal form.

we can be by the grace of God is certainly satisfying for today. At the same time, a hope that does not reach beyond time into eternity is a pitiful and miserable comforter when we most need comfort.

Without the expansion of the resurrection, our hope becomes dim and dull. It narrows down into some vague idea of soul survival or some indefinite concept of immortality. Have you ever wondered how you would feel if one morning you got up and looked at yourself in the mirror and there was no face in the reflection? Kind of scary, would not you say? Without the resurrection, the hope of life after death becomes faceless, an impersonal hope of diminished survival in some kind of ethereal form.

The resurrection gives the hope of life after death palpability and a tangible quality. Our eternal destiny is not a disembodied spirit in limbo, but a new and glorified body that is similar to our Lord's post-resurrection body. The disciples believed in some form of soul survival and were frightened and powerless men before the resurrection. It was the tangibility of the resurrection, which extended the dimension of their hoping far beyond the tyranny of time.

In 2 Timothy 1:10, we read that the appearing of Christ has "destroyed death and has brought life and immortality to light through the gospel." Christ brought out of the shadows this concept of *Sheol*, a place where disembodied spirits barely survived in a state of half-life, into the light of resurrection glory. It is like taking a negative where the faces are a ghostly gray and reproducing it in living color.

Without the resurrection, we might just as well write over our preaching, our believing and our hoping the words of Ecclesiastes:

"all *is* vanity and grasping for the wind" (Eccl. 1:14 NKJV), or, just so much hot air. I wonder if those who deny the resurrection, who feel it is a myth, or who spiritualize it away to the point that it has no meaning, are prepared to face the consequences of their denial?

The Glorious Reality of the Positive

The negative need not overwhelm us. Paul goes beyond the "what if" to exclaim in 1 Corinthians 15:20: "But Christ has indeed been raised from the dead . . ." Here is an inspired affirmation that rings true with the perfect pitch of confident assurance. He is risen *indee*d and not just in theory or in the idealism of religious symbolism. There is, therefore, point and power to our preaching, substance and support to our believing, and reason and justification for our hoping. Because He is risen, we can preach, believe, and hope to our heart's content.

> Because Christ is risen, there is point and power to our preaching, substance and support to our believing, and reason and justification for our hoping.

In light of Easter dawning, we can answer in the affirmative: is there sufficient power for me to turn my pessimism into praise? Can I rise above the cynical, secular humanism of this world? Can I overcome the selfish values of me, mine, and more and live life to the glory of Thee, Thine, and Your will be done?

Yes, to all these questions. "For Christ has indeed been raised from the dead, the firstfruits of those who have fallen asleep" (1 Cor. 15:20). The seed sleeps in the earth until it dies, and springs to new life and lifts its sprout, which becomes a shaft, a bladed shaft and, finally, a head ripe for harvest. The first sheaves of ripened grain are cut down and the cuttings brought to the temple in anticipation of a full harvest. The Hebrew farmer takes that shock of wheat and waves it before the Lord in celebration of nature's pledge that a full harvest is on the way. In like manner, the rising of our Savior is God's guarantee that: "as in Adam all die, so in Christ will all be made alive" (1 Cor. 15:22). A full harvest of eternal life is on the way for all who are in Christ. That is the consummation of our praise and the source of our sense of humor.

Finally, What About the Napkin?

John's Gospel informs us that the napkin used to cover the face of Jesus was folded up and placed to the side. What a striking detail. Could it have some deeper, symbolic meaning? In the etiquette of the time, when the master of the house had finished supper, he would take the napkin and carefully wipe his face and his beard. Lying on the table all crumpled up, it was a signal to the servers that he had finished his meal and it was time to clear the table and wash the dishes. If he were to leave the table and keep his napkin neatly folded up, it was an indication he had not finished eating and would be returning to the table.

Was this little detail Jesus' way of saying: "I am not finished, I will be returning to the table of Communion and there you will find me in the broken bread and the shared cup?" When you are dining at a restaurant and your server removes your dishes but leaves your fork, you know the best is yet to come—desert is on the menu. Like that fork, this folded napkin is a marvelous metaphor indicating *the best is yet to come*. As we saw in the first sign: "You have saved the best wine until now."

NINE

Post-Resurrection Postscript

A Power That Turns Failure and Frustration into the Gladness of Fulfillment

Afterward Jesus appeared again to his disciples, by the Sea of Galilee. It happened this way: Simon Peter, Thomas (also known as Didymus), Nathanael from Cana in Galilee, the sons of Zebedee,and two other disciples were together. "I'm going out to fish," Simon Peter told them, and they said, "We'll go with you." So they went out and got into the boat, but that night they caught nothing.

Early in the morning, Jesus stood on the shore, but the disciples did not realize that it was Jesus.

He called out to them, "Friends, haven't you any fish?"

"No," they answered.

He said, "Throw your net on the right side of the boat and you will find some." When they did, they were unable to haul the net in because of the large number of fish.

Then the disciple whom Jesus loved said to Peter, "It is the Lord!" As soon as Simon Peter heard him say, "It is the Lord," he wrapped his outer garment around him (for he had taken it off) and jumped into the water. The other disciples followed in the boat, towing the net full of fish, for they were not far from shore, about a hundred yards. When they landed, they saw a fire of burning coals there with fish on it, and some bread.

Jesus said to them, "Bring some of the fish you have just caught." So Simon Peter climbed back into the boat and dragged the net ashore. It was full of large fish, 153, but even with so many the net was not torn. Jesus said to them, "Come and have breakfast." None of the disciples dared ask him, "Who are you?" They knew it was the Lord. Jesus came, took the bread and gave it to them, and did the same with the fish. This was now the third time Jesus appeared to his disciples after he was raised from the dead.

(John 21:1–14)

Breakfast on the Beach

I remember it as if it were yesterday. It was the dawn of Easter Sunday, April 6, 1969, in a military compound outside a little town called Tuy Hoa, South Viet Nam. Arising before the sun, I, another chaplain, and an assistant, carried three large wooden crosses to a strip of beach that had been prepared beforehand. We made long trails in the sand as we dragged the crosses along to a place just beyond the surf. Leaning those crosses into a brisk breeze blowing in from the South China Sea, we planted them in the sand. The soldiers sat on logs that had been laid by combat engineers as we celebrated an unforgettable Easter sunrise service. We chaplains stood on wooden pallets with our backs toward the eastern horizon. We saw the morning light reflected in the young faces of the troops. For

> As we celebrated an unforgettable Easter sunrise service, the morning light was reflected in the young faces of the troops.

our Scripture reading, we chose this passage in John twenty-one, which we entitled, "Sunrise on the Beach."

It seemed to fit the occasion so well. Seven apostles sat in a fishing boat on the Sea of Galilee. They had been there all night. As the light of dawn was breaking, a stranger stood on shore and called to them. "Friends, haven't you any fish?" His voice traveled effortlessly over the water.

They answered, "No.

He said, "Throw your net on the right side of the boat and you will find some."

Had I been one of these seven fishermen/disciples, I would have been tempted to think, *What does this stranger know? I have fished this lake all my adult life. I know the best places and techniques. Why should I move the nets and spook any school of fish that might be moving into the area?* But there was something vaguely familiar about that voice. It had a tone of authority. So they did what He said. And, wouldn't you know it, the moving of the net seemed to attract every fish in the lake. Their net enclosed such a catch they were unable to drag it onboard.

John the Beloved, with characteristic spiritual insight, was the first to realize, "It is the Lord!"

Peter, with characteristic impulsiveness, casts himself into the water and begins swimming for shore. The others struggle with the difficult task of rowing that net full of flopping fish one hundred yards back to the beach.

What a scene for some gifted painter to immortalize on canvas.

As Peter emerges, dripping wet from the fresh water, there is no longer any doubt. As verse twelve puts it, "None of the disciples dared ask him, 'Who are you?' They knew it was the Lord."

Peter may have realized for the very first time that this same Jesus could no longer be an obscure Jewish rabbi who once lived and taught in Palestine. He is risen above class, caste, clan and creed to become the Savior of the world.

The Cosmic Christ

We were a cross-section of humanity demonstrating that the Christ of the empty tomb belongs to the whole world—He is universal.

That was the conviction that came upon two chaplains and an assistant as we stood on that strand of beach in Phou Diep province. We saw it reflected in the faces of those who sat on the logs. In one section there was a large group of ROK (Republic of Korea) troops with their Korean chaplain. In another section there was a big group of ARVN (Army of the Republic of Viet Nam) troops with their chaplain. Sprinkled throughout were Americans of ethnic diversity and of all ranks and military specialties. They were all looking to the eastern horizon and the One who is risen above continents and cultures to become the Cosmic Christ, the Lord of all. We were more than a small colony of Americans who had banded together to practice a foreign religion on alien soil. We were a cross-section of humanity demonstrating that the Christ of the empty tomb belongs to the whole world—He is universal.

Christ and Culture

Often people make the mistake of equating Christ with Western culture. In 1970, I heard Dr. Dick West, a renowned artist of Indian ancestry and teacher at Bacon College. In interpreting some of his paintings, he made the statement that many of our religious concepts come from European art of the Middle Ages. The European masters never painted Jesus as a Jew of the first century but as an Italian or a Spaniard of their own time and place. These classical art forms have become hardened into lifeless stereotypes, thus making Christianity foreign and alien to other cultures. His mission was to paint Christ as a Native American for Native Americans.

I was especially interested in his painting of the Last Supper. The scene takes place in a teepee rather than an upper room. The disciples are sitting cross-legged on animal skins rather than at a table. They are passing a peace pipe, rather than a cup. The Christ figure is making a "V-sign which means, "One of you will speak with a forked tongue."

> In every season and situation of life, holy humor is the appropriate response to resurrection majesty.

Here was a man who had caught the vision of a universal Christ and was using his artistic gifts to make that reality more meaningful to his people. Many of the petty prejudices and the silly divisions which plague Protestants would be healed if we could have our minds stretched by the universality of our Savior. "Let everything that has breath praise the Lord" (Ps. 150:6).

The resurrection has given our praise a cosmic quality that makes it real and relevant in every nation under heaven. In every season and situation of life, holy humor is the appropriate response to resurrection majesty.

As I stood on the beach in Viet Nam with my back toward the rising sun and my face toward the smiling, upturned faces of the troops, I felt like laughing at Lucifer. He was laughing on Good Friday. He had won. Jesus was dead. "It is finished," moaned the dying Christ.

But the empty tomb turned the tables on the Evil One. The work of redeeming man to God was indeed finished, but the life-giving Spirit of Jesus was just beginning. On Easter Sunday Jesus got the last laugh, and He who laughs last, laughs best.

I believe that same principle of heavenly happiness extends throughout the whole universe into galaxies light years away. I like to call it the Comic Spirit of redemption.

I needed to follow the liturgy prepared for the Easter sunrise service, but I felt like chanting, with a chuckle in my voice:

> "Death has been swallowed up in victory. Where, O death, is your victory? Where, O death, is your sting?" The sting of death is sin, and the power of sin is the law. But thanks be to God! who gives us the victory through our Lord Jesus Christ.
> (1 Cor. 15:55–57)

Many scholars regard this as part of an Easter hymn sung by the church of the first century, which mocks and laughs at Satan. When Jesus cried out; "My God, my God why have you forsaken me?" (Matt. 27:46), Satan laughed gleefully. At last, God's Son is forsaken and swallowed up by the grave. But the empty tomb with the stone rolled away opened the mouth for Satan to be sucked in. That's Dante's *Divine Comedy*—the swallower has been swallowed. That's the big joke the resurrection pulled on the Prince of Darkness.

The Christ of the Commonplace

Another conviction that dawned on me that Easter sunrise of 1969 was: our Cosmic Christ who has risen above nationalism, tribalism and every other "ism" that would divide man from man, has not risen above the commonplace. He has risen above death and decay but not above the daily drudgery, the mundane monotony, and the repetitious routine of life.

The last verse of our Scripture passage identifies this as the third resurrection appearance. The previous two, as recorded by John, took place in Jerusalem on successive Sunday evenings as the disciples were gathered together in the upper room to conduct a worship service. This third one is in a class by itself. It occurred not on Sunday, but on a weekday; not in the sacred city, but in Galilee as they were out on the lake practicing their trade. The angels that guarded the tomb

> Christ meets us on our own ground. We can reach Him in the most familiar facets of life.

caught the same spirit; "He has risen from the dead and is going ahead of you into Galilee. There you will see him" (Matt. 28:7). Galilee was the most familiar place in the entire world to them. They had grown up in the towns dotting the western shore of the lake. There they had lived most of their adult lives. Always He goes before us into our Galilee where He meets us on our own ground. We can reach Him in the most familiar facets of life.

We can praise the Lord that our Risen Christ cannot be contained in an upper room or even a sacred city. Nor can He be limited to one day of the week. All too many think Sunday is the only day to seek the Lord and the church is the only place to find him. This twenty-first chapter of Matthew reminds us He is with us not only on Sundays as we gather for worship, but also through the week as we scatter for service.

As they were about the routine of earning their livelihood, Jesus revealed Himself to them. Often we take the familiar things for granted. We look for the divine in the unusual and the dramatic. In birth, marriage, danger, and death we turn to God. Are these mountain peaks of crises the only time to find God? How about the wide valleys in between where we live most of our lives? Is He not there behind the desk, on top of that pile of reports, in that sink of dirty dishes?

The Christ of crises is also the Christ of the commonplace.

Our Galilee is in those multiplied moments of the mundane with which we struggle: balancing our checkbooks, finding employment, living on a fixed income, and preparing for retirement. He "is going ahead of you" into all these things and there you shall find Him. The Christ of crises is also the Christ of the commonplace. When we meet him in our Galilee, we are bound to have a John twenty-one experience. This is good news for those of us who wish to be delivered from daily drudgery. The secret of rising out of our ruts is to recognize, "It is the Lord!"

This is a secret we should blab to the world. There are, of course, certain secrets we should guard, lest we throw our "pearls to pigs" (Matt. 7:6). Jesus counseled us to enter our rooms and pray to our Father in secret (Matt. 6:6). There are confessions people have shared with us in confidence that we hold in the closet of strictest secrecy.

But there is something we must come out of our rooms and confess to a world that often takes itself too seriously. It is this: Discovering the Christ of the commonplace and the common people in every circumstance is to open the door to a lighthearted levity that inspires laughter. When it comes to that, I just can't keep the secret. The sweet fragrance of that breakfast cooking over hot coals is just too good to remain silent. I just can't help myself.

Father James Martin in his book, *Between Heaven and Mirth,* spices it up with delightful humor, which reflects his life as a Jesuit priest. One of my favorites is:

We must confess to the world that discovering the Christ of the commonplace opens the door to a lighthearted levity that inspires laughter.

A Diocesan Priest, a Franciscan friar, a Benedictine priest, a Trappist monk, and a Jesuit priest are about to start a group retreat together. Since they're going to be sharing some personal matters with one another during their group meetings, they decide to start off by building trust: they will discuss their worst failings on the first day. They will do so in strict confidence, so that everyone can feel free to speak honestly. The parish priest goes first. "Well, my brothers," he says, "thank God this is confidential, because my sin is so embarrassing. I hate to say this, but I just don't pray. I know it's part of my priestly life, but prayer can be so dry. Oh, I'm so embarrassed. But I'm happy that we can be honest and so glad this is all confidential—I would be horrified if anyone knew!"

Then the Franciscan friar says, "Oh, brothers, my sin is more embarrassing than that. Sometimes when I get a donation for the community, I don't turn it in as I should. I keep it for myself, even though it's against my vow of poverty. I feel better about sharing this, but thank God this is confidential!"

Then the Benedictine says, "Oh brothers, my sin is far worse. I teach liturgy at our local Benedictine college, but I miss mass all the time. Sometime I'm so busy grading papers in the morning that I can't go to mass. I couldn't imagine what would happen if my abbot knew this. But I feel better telling you this in confidence.

Then the Trappist says, "Brothers, my sin is far, far worse, and I'm much more embarrassed! We monks are supposed to stay in the monastery all the time, but every few days I sneak out and go to the movies. I'm covered in shame. Thank God this is all confidential."

All the while the Jesuit sits quietly. Finally, one of them says to him, "Father?" And the Jesuit says, "Oh brothers, my sin is the worst of all . . . I just can't keep a secret!"[21]

---

[21]   Martin, James, S. J., *Between Heaven and Mirth: Why Joy, Humor, and Laughter are at the Heart of the Spiritual Life.* (New York: Harper Collins,), pp. 193—194.

Here's a secret: joy humor and laughter help us to experience God's presence in our daily lives.

The Same Jesus in a Sublime Body

> Jesus bothered with breakfast because His friends were hungry and He was concerned.

In His new body, Jesus was not above serving breakfast to seven hungry fishermen. I find that catches me by surprise and inspires a smile. I might have expected him to be too absorbed with the problems of the universe to bother with something as menial as preparing a meal. In His resurrected state, He had a glorified body that was immune from hunger and no longer required physical nourishment. Why should He bother with breakfast? Because His friends were hungry and He was concerned. It's really that simple.

Breakfast on the beach with the Immortal One as host! Those kind and considerate words, "Come and have breakfast," were like music in the ears of these wet and weary men of the sea. Imagine how famished they were after a night of fruitless labor. Those fish frying on an open fire and that bread warming on hot coals must have smelled heavenly. Nothing tastes as good as food cooked in the out-of-doors.

My intention is not to make you hungry but to illustrate the truth that, even after the resurrection, Jesus was not above getting down to where people are and ministering to their physical needs. Jesus had gone through a crucifixion and a resurrection but he was still the same person he had always been. The cross had taken His blood and the resurrection had equipped Him with a glorified body, but nothing could change His heart. They nailed him to a cross and pierced His heart with a spear but they could not destroy His personality. He was still the same wonderful person they had known; intensely concerned for them and their immediate need, whatever it might be, spiritual or physical.

The church often gives people the impression it is only interested in their soul—that as long as a person's soul is saved, it doesn't matter what happens to his body. He can live in a ghetto or a state of poverty—the important thing is that he's got religion in his heart. In giving this impression, the church has misrepresented the Christ who said to His disciples, "Gather 'round boys, first we'll have a bite of breakfast and then we'll talk religion."

That's the Hoffman translation that is not inspired. Some people might consider it a reversed vision, rather than a revised version.

> Jesus after the cross and the resurrection was the same wonderful person the disciples had known—intensely concerned for them and their needs.

But there is an inspired truth here that the church has yet to grasp. Jesus was not about to send Peter out to feed His sheep spiritual food until He had first fed him breakfast. Jesus is concerned for all our needs as He demonstrated so convincingly in this postscript of John's Gospel.

"Whatever You Did For One of the Least . . ."

Again, I flash back to Tuy Hoa. After our sunrise service on the beach, we went to the combat support hospital's mess hall and had breakfast, then carried trays to wounded soldiers. Then, after all the services were over, we loaded up a bus with G.I.s and went to the Catholic orphanage in the town of Tuy Hoa. I watched in amazement as the soldiers painted walls, repaired equipment, held children, talked to the sisters, and performed many useful tasks. Combat-hardened faces somehow became softer as "horseback" rides were given to children squealing with delight.

> We had made contact with the Christ of the commonplace as we went about doing those common tasks for others.

I thought I could hear Jesus say, "Whatever you did for one of the least of these brothers of mine, you did for me" (Matt. 25:40). As the shadows began to lengthen one of the sergeants said, "Padre, we need to get back." The road belonged to "Charlie" after dark. So, we loaded up and headed back to our compound. Everybody was in such high spirits. Some brave soul started singing, "Up from the grave he a-rose . . ." and soon over half the bus was chiming in on, "Lo, in the grave he lay, Jesus my Savior, waiting the coming day, Jesus my Lord . . ."

It was a magic moment. The hair on the back of my neck was standing straight out and my body was covered with Holy Ghost goose bumps. No one dared ask, "Is this Easter?" They all seemed to know the Living Lord was riding home with them on that bus. We had somehow made contact with the Christ of the commonplace and the common people as we went about doing these common tasks for others.

The "Eternal" Night of Failure

Our cosmic Christ, who is also the Christ of the commonplace, is our contemporary. John 21:1 says, "Afterward Jesus appeared again to his disciples . . ." I like to add: *again* and *again* and yet *again*. This is a prophetic page out of the past that proclaims what Christ is doing in the present. As such, it is as current as tomorrow's headlines.

For instance, have you ever felt like a failure? Can you hear the tone of failure in Peter's voice as he says, "I'm going out to fish." Perhaps he was thinking, *Let's face it, I'll never make it as a disciple. I denied him three times when He needed me the most. The standards are too high; I'll never measure up. But, I can still fish with the best of them.* But after a long lonely night of futility, he must have been doubly devastated. *Not only can I not catch men for the kingdom, I can't even catch fish anymore, not even a little minnow.*

> When the chips were down, the disciples didn't have the guts to stand with Jesus.

It's bad enough to fish for fun and catch nothing. When you are depending on it for a livelihood, it can be downright depressing. But there is something deeper here than just a failure to catch fish. This long night on the Sea of Galilee served to remind them of their greater failure in following Christ. When Jesus first met them by the shores of this lake three years previously, He called them to discipleship with these words: "Come, follow me," . . . "and I will make you fishers of men" (Matt. 4:19). How many men had they caught for the kingdom? How closely had they followed Him into the deepening shadows of the cross? When He was arrested in the Garden of Gethsemane, they forsook Him and fled. When the chips were down, they didn't have the guts to stand with Him.

Of all the disciples, Peter was the most aware of his failure. He had been the most insistent in pledging his loyalty. He vowed publicly that he would die rather than deny his Lord. He had overestimated his own courage and was deeply ashamed that he was not the man he thought he was or would like to be. A sense of utter and complete failure came upon him and his companions.

The Emerging Light of Fulfillment

At the dawning of a new day, this vaguely familiar voice came to them across the water, "Friends, haven't you any fish?" ("How is it going, have

> It's amazing how successful people can be when they do things God's way, acting in obedience to the word of Christ.

you caught anything?") They freely confessed they hadn't. And suddenly, Jesus was there to turn their long and lonely night of failure into a new day of fulfillment.

Psalms 30:5 puts this story to music: "Weeping may remain for a night, but rejoicing comes in the morning." We've all had nights when we have felt engulfed in the gloom of total failure. Like Peter, many of us have had nights when we have denied our Savior and felt the guilt and shame of it; nights when we reverted back to our old lives because we felt we couldn't make the grade as a Christian and why go on pretending; nights when we have compromised our convictions for popularity or pleasure.

Those nights are not eternal. At the breaking of day, the Christ of Easter dawning comes to us and "with healing in His wings" (Mal. 4:2 NKJV). Like these disciples on Lake Galilee, we too can find Him in frustration and failure.

What a difference it made when they heard His word and put His divine directive into action. Their empty net got so full of fish, one hundred and fifty-three by actual count, that it should have torn and spilled its precious catch back into the lake. It wasn't made for that many fish, but somehow it held together.

What a parabolic picture! It's amazing how successful people can be when they do things God's way acting in obedience to the word of Christ. When God fills our empty lives with His abundance, no matter how much He gives

> God knows how to fill your life with big fish and big cause, and keep you from breaking under the pressure.

us, no matter how much it stretches us, everything holds together. The people who are coming apart at the seams are doing so not because their lives are too full, but because they are too empty. It's not because they've got hold of something so big they wonder if they can handle it. It's because they feel unchallenged, unused, pushed aside, with nothing for which to live. God knows how to fill your life with big fish and big causes and, at the same time, keep you from breaking under the pressure. Isn't that a cause for laughter?

Divine Directives Are Not Always Logical

Sometimes the word that comes to us makes just about as much sense as: "Throw your net on the right side of the boat." Any fisherman knows one side of the boat is just as good as the other. Stirring up the water will only drive the fish away. All I can tell you is, whatever He says, do it, no matter how illogical it may sound. When you implement His word in an act of obedience that is inspired by faith, it will make all the difference. It will turn your failure into a new day of fulfillment. How can we not "be of good cheer" about such a power that finds us in our moments of utter futility and turns our fruitlessness into fulfillment (John 16:33 NKJV)?

"Yes, there is healing power in humor," says Lois H. Morgan of Mocksville, North Carolina, who wrote the following poem "after a very dark depression."

Jesus,
I believe you laughed
As Mary bathed you
And Joseph tickled your toes.
I believe you giggled
As you and other children
Played your childhood games.
And when you went
To the temple
And astounded the teachers,
I believe you chuckled
As all children chuckle
When they stump adults.
And surely there were
Moments of merriment
As you and your disciples
Deepened your relationship.
And as you and Mary
And Martha and Lazarus
Fellowshipped, mirth
Must have been mirrored
On your faces.
Jesus,
I know you wept
And anguished. But
I believe you laughed, too.
Create in me
The life of laughter.[22]

---

[22]   Lois H. Morgan, quoted by (Carl and Rose Samra Samra, *Holy Humor, Inspirational Wit, and Cartoons*, 238—239). Used by permission.

Sidelights and Insights That Highlight a Power That Produces a Sense of Humor

When they had finished eating, Jesus said to Simon Peter, "Simon son of John, do you love me more than these?"

"Yes, Lord," he said, "you know that I love you."

Jesus said, "Feed my lambs."

Again Jesus said, "Simon son of John, do you love me?"

He answered, "Yes, Lord, you know that I love you."

Jesus said, "Take care of my sheep."

The third time he said to him, "Simon son of John, do you love me?" Peter was hurt because Jesus asked him the third time, "Do you love me?" He said, "Lord, you know all things; you know that I love you." Jesus said, "Feed my sheep. Very truly I tell you, when you were younger you dressed yourself and went where you wanted; but when you are old you will stretch out your hands, and someone else will dress you and lead you where you do not want to go." Jesus said this to indicate the kind of death by which Peter would glorify God. Then he said to him, "Follow me!"

Peter turned and saw that the disciple whom Jesus loved was following them. (This was the one who had leaned back against Jesus at the supper and had said, "Lord, who is going to betray you?") When Peter saw him, he asked, "Lord, what about him?"

Jesus answered, "If I want him to remain alive until I return, what is that to you? You must follow me." Because of this, the rumor spread among the believers that this disciple would not die. But Jesus did not say that he would not die; he only said, "If I want him to remain alive until I return, what is that to you?"

This is the disciple who testifies to these things and who wrote them down. We know that his testimony is true.

Jesus did many other things as well. If every one of them were written down, I suppose that even the whole world would not have room for the books that would be written.
(John 21:15–25)

Throughout this book our prayer has been that we "might know Christ and the power of his resurrection" (Phil. 3:10). His resurrection power is purposeful. One of its primary purposes is to produce lovely laughter in the life of the believer. It is continually working toward this end. In this closing section we want to look at some interesting sidelights, which otherwise might be missed.

A Conclusion That Does Not Conclude

Did you notice how neatly and concisely John, the Beloved Apostle, concludes the fourth Gospel?

Jesus did many other miraculous signs in the presence of his disciples, which are not recorded in this book. But these are written that you may believe that Jesus is the Christ, the Son of God, and that by believing you may have life in his name.
(John 20:30–31)

What a wonderful concluding statement! The purpose of the book is summarized and all the loose ends are neatly tied together. When you read it you want to say, "The end." Why then this *twenty-first* chapter? It seems rather anticlimactic. Some scholars believe it was added some time later as an appendix to deal with some important problems that had arisen among the first- century believers. These perplexing problems present us with some fascinating sidelights which reflect what Christians were thinking two thousand years ago.

What Did Jesus Really Say?

One of those sidelights is regarding John himself and his advancing age. It is likely, by the time the twenty-first chapter was written that all the apostles save John had died a martyr's death. Only John was left. Would he be the only one to die a natural death? Or would he die at all? Perhaps he would survive until Jesus returned? A rumor got started based upon a misunderstanding of what Jesus had said on His third post-resurrection appearance.

The rumor is reported this way. "Because of this, the rumor spread among the brothers that this disciple would not die" (John 21:23). You can imagine how all eyes turned to the state of John's health. If he caught cold and sneezed, it sent reverberations throughout all the churches. Don't you find a subtle humor in that?

Jesus had not said He would not die. What Jesus said was, "If I want him to remain alive until I return, what is that to you?" This twenty-first chapter was appended later to set the record straight and report what Jesus had actually said on that occasion.

Isn't that a fascinating sidelight upon first-century faith? The early Christians were not immune to misunderstandings and every effort was made by the apostles to correct them when they arose. It was vitally important to the early church to know exactly what Jesus really said and interpret it correctly. Jesus claimed on several occasions that He would come again in a glorious second appearing to consummate the kingdom. But he stubbornly refused to set any date. In spite of that, throughout the centuries sincere believers have attempted to set dates and make predictions. Every time that happens we can be sure it is a misunderstanding of what Jesus really said.

If we are to be successful in developing a lifestyle of laughter, it is essential we know exactly what Jesus said, not what some charismatic leader *says* Jesus said. It is so tempting to get sidetracked by rumor or some current fad circulating through the church.

The disciple of holy humor needs to focus upon what Jesus actually said and pray for the wisdom to interpret it in a responsible way.

When we were younger, many of us felt confident that we would live to see the return of Christ in our generation. Most of us have not completely given up on the possibility of that happening. But, at the same time, we recognize Jesus didn't say He would return at the close of the twentieth century, the beginning of the third millennium, or any other specific time. What He said was, "I will come again, and receive you unto myself; that where I am there ye may be also" (John 14:3 KJV). That is the light at the end of the tunnel that keeps us going, growing, and even glowing with the joy of anticipation. It is not rumor, but *rhema*, meaning in Greek an authentic word from the Lord that inspires faith in our hearts and keeps our mirth burning brightly.

Living a Stretched-Out Life

Another interesting sidelight shines upon Peter, and how Jesus predicted the way he should glorify God by a martyr's death. "When you were younger you dressed yourself and went where you wanted; but when you are old you will stretch out your hands, and someone else will dress you and lead you where you do not want to go" (John 21:18).

According to tradition, that's exactly how Peter died, stretching out his hands on a cross in the city of Rome. Tradition tells us he insisted on being crucified upside down because he felt unworthy to be crucified right

> If we want to glorify God in our dying, we better start glorifying God in our living, and the sooner the better.

side up, as was his Lord. We can take that historical sidelight and turn it into an insight. Jesus' word to Peter not only predicted the kind of death he would die, it proclaimed the kind of life he would live in stretching his hands and his heart out to God in praise. If we want to glorify God in our dying, we better start glorifying God in our living, and the sooner the better. One of the ways we can do that is to reach out toward our full potential and live a stretched-out life to the glory of God.

If Our Foresight Were as Clear as Our Hindsight, Our Insight Would Be a Lot Clearer

John 21:18 opens up the exercise of hindsight: "When you were younger you dressed yourself and went where you wanted." In our youth we were often dazzled by the deception of our own sufficiency. We were masters of our fate. We could go here and there and do what we wanted, whenever we wanted. We were indestructible!

With hindsight, many of us can look back on periods of arrogant pride. As we exercise foresight, we can see that life is moving us in the same direction as Peter—from self-sufficiency to surrender. Death itself is the final act of yielding as we leave everything behind and go on to God.

Open-handed humor helps us to die to self and live to the glory of God.

As we learn from hindsight and exercise foresight, we come to the insight that the best way to prepare for the inevitable is to learn how to relinquish control, to open our hands, and to stretch out our arms in the art of surrender. When we make a fist, all we can do is fight and defend ourselves. An open-handed humor helps us to die to self and live to the glory of God.

Three's the Charm

> By a charcoal fire, Peter fell. By another, of our Lord's kindling, he would be restored.

There is one other interesting sidelight we are apt to miss that shows our Lord's close attention to detail. John 21:9 speaks of "a fire of burning coals." In only one other place in the gospel of John is a charcoal fire mentioned—John 18:18. It was there in the courtyard of the high priest that Peter warmed himself before he denied knowing Jesus or having ever been associated with him.

By a charcoal fire Peter fell. By another, of our Lord's kindling, he would be restored. Three times—the third time with cursing and swearing—he had denied Christ. Three times the Risen One called and commissioned him to, "Feed my lambs," "Tend my sheep," "Shepherd my flock." That's our Lord's way of saying "I have seen your tears of repentance, I know you are genuinely sorry for your sins and your healing is complete."

Before Peter was reinstated by the Risen One, he must have felt he had forever disqualified himself from any kind of leadership. We can turn a page or two in our Bibles to the first chapter of Acts. The one hundred and twenty are in the upper room before the day of Pentecost. They are looking for a replacement for Judas. A psalm is quoted which is applied to the betrayer, "May another take his place of leadership" (Acts 1:20). Before his restoration, Peter would have applied this verse to himself. In denying his Lord, Peter felt just as guilty as

> We have all denied Christ in one way or another. If we have "wept bitterly" tears of remorse, we have been restored.

Judas who betrayed him. *Let someone else take my office, I am no longer worthy.*

Doubtless, others disciples agreed. *Peter can no longer lead us; he has proven himself unworthy!* A crisis of leadership may have developed in the church. This inspired appendix was written to show Peter was fit to lead. He had been fully restored by Christ Himself and recommissioned for service.

Like Peter, we have all denied Christ in one way or another. Like Peter, have we "wept bitterly" tears of remorse? If we have, then also like Peter, we have been restored.

> Like Peter, we need healing from the inside out or we can never be of service to Christ.

Once I clung to the myth that it was the non-Christian world that was hurting. Christians should have it all together. I've come to see this is a deception that turns people in their brokenness away from the church. The church is not a hotel for saints; it is a hospital for sinners. It is a place of healing for the walking wounded. Christians are hurting as much as anyone else, in some ways more, because the Holy Spirit has quickened our conscience to be sensitive to things that may not bother others. Like Peter, we need healing from the inside out or we can never be of service to Christ. This is true because the fundamental requirement in any form of Christian service is reinstatement and the forgiveness that accompanies it.

We serve a miraculous Christ as we have seen throughout this book. With all that power, it is hard for us to understand why He allows us to fall and to fail. Like Peter, at times, we even deny Him by our attitudes and actions. He allows it in order to restore us for more effective service through His forgiving love. Rehabilitation is a vital part of our Lord's program of preparation.

The Motive of Service

> Unless love for Jesus is the major motivational thrust behind how hard we work, it is not Christian service.

No matter how hard we work, unless love for Jesus is the major motivational thrust behind it and within it, it is not Christian service. It may be humanitarian, it may be socially beneficial, it may even be sacrificial; but unless it is an extension of our personal devotion to Jesus as our special friend, it is not specifically Christian.

"Simon son of John, do you truly love me more than these?" (John 21:15).

In asking this question three times, our Lord reveals what He wants most from us: not primarily our time, talent, or treasure, but our feelings of affection.

Notice, He did not ask, "Are you a seminary graduate, do you have all kinds of degrees after your name, are you blessed with a body beautiful or a charming personality, a sparkling wit or a gift of gab?"

Of course, God can use all these special qualities if they are yielded to Him. But the crucial question has always been, "Do you really, genuinely love me?"

Get ready! One day we will meet Him face to face and He will have a question for us. The One who asks knows our hearts better than we know ourselves. Like Peter may we affirm, "Yes, Lord, you know that I love you."

Our Marching Orders

We can take our highlighter again and accentuate our mission. Here is a concise expression of it, three times repeated for emphasis. "Feed my sheep."

I see tending as a broader concept than just feeding. The shepherd doesn't really feed sheep. He leads them to pasture and they go to work feeding themselves. So many want to be spoon fed the Gospel. The shepherd cannot do that. He can only lead the sheep to the most nourishing pasture and turn them loose to graze. Good Bible teaching and preaching are vitally important. But, dear reader, there are things you must do for yourself in getting your nose buried in the Bible and thoroughly digesting what you read.

In tending the sheep, the shepherd provides another vital function by keeping them together as a flock. After spreading out in green pastures all day long, as the shadows begin to lengthen, it's time to gather the sheep together before returning to the safety and security of the fold. The Palestinian shepherd calls his sheep by name as we would a domesticated pet. He recognizes their individual traits and they come when he calls. They huddle together around their shepherd before returning to the fold. Anyone can scatter sheep. Only the shepherd can cause them to press in and gather strength and warmth from one another.

The message of the Shepherd is: it's time to pack tightly together and move back to the shelter of the sheepfold with our Good Shepherd in the center of everything we do, say, think and feel.

Cowboy or Shepherd?

The power we feel flowing through the Gospel of John is "shepherd power." The prophet Isaiah caught the essence of it. "He tends his flock like a shepherd: he gathers the lambs in his arms and carries them close to his heart; he gently leads those that have young" (Isa. 40:11).

The shepherd is a leader. His leadership style is characterized by gentleness. That may be foreign to some of us. Those who have been influenced by western culture are much more in tune with the image of the cowboy. The cowboy drives the herd to market. The shepherd leads

The shepherd's leadership style is characterized by gentleness, in contrast to the cowboy's.

the sheep to pasture. They are as different as night and day. The smoking gun, whistling rope, and flashing spurs, are foreign to the tools of the shepherd. He depends only on a "rod" to drive away predators and a "staff" to gently touch the flanks of the sheep and guide them back into the flock. He never uses a branding iron because he recognizes the unique characteristics of each individual sheep.

Like sheep, people tend to scatter in confusion when they are driven. They resent being branded and brainwashed by the secular values of a godless culture. They need a shepherd who knows the way and can gently lead them by the persuasive power of a positive example. That is the power of our Good Shepherd that He uses in leading us to "green pastures" of contentment and "still waters" of serenity. We need never tire of smiling for the joy which flows in our lives when we can say, "The Lord is *my* Shepherd."

The Danger of Distraction

In addition to our motive and mission, we have a clear mandate which is repeated twice. "Follow me." In highlighting it, let this scene capture our imagination. Peter is walking side by side with the Risen One along a strip of beach on the western shore of Lake Galilee. Jesus has just revealed to him how he should glorify God in his martyrdom.

Peter can't resist it. Looking back over his shoulder, he sees John walking behind them a few paces. He just has to ask, "Lord, what about him?" Is he going to live to a ripe old age, is he going to die a natural death, or what?

"What is that to you? You must follow me," our Lord replies.

In other words, don't be distracted by what I have planned for someone else, you've got all you can handle just to follow your own destiny.

I can think of no better way to conclude this book on the power of holy humor, than to highlight this lesson. Too often in our service we allow ourselves to be distracted by what God is doing through other people in other places. The fact is, we have all we can handle just to follow Christ and be true to the unique calling He has for each of us. How much more merriment would be generated by each child of God if we would, without diversion, direct our undivided attention to the primary task of following Christ, loving Him, and listening to Him.

Conclusion

Throughout this book I have tried to let all the signs point to the person of Christ who has the power to enable us to turn our frowns into smiles. We cannot do that in our own strength. We need the power of His resurrection to create a lifestyle of holy humor. By faith we can tap into the Christ of miracles and the miracles of Christ and find them sufficient for our needs.

I leave you with the lame man who sat begging at "the temple gate called Beautiful" (Acts 3:1–10). We see ourselves reflected in that man. He was sitting outside not able to pass through the Beautiful gate into the temple and render his praise to God. His feet and ankle bones could not support the weight of his body. But, in an act of faith, Peter reached down and took him by the right hand.

> He helped him up, and instantly the man's feet and ankles became strong. He jumped to his feet and began to walk. Then he went with them into the temple courts, walking and jumping and praising God. (Acts 3:7)

No wonder the people were "filled with wonder and amazement."

By faith in the Risen One, we can receive miraculous power to rise from our pallets of pessimism and walk the path of praise, at times leaping for joy with the precious privilege of making our incomparable Jesus the subject of our exultation.

Living Lord, we remember you were not born in a cathedral between two candles. Nor were you placed in a palace on a gilded pillow, for royalty to adore. O Christ of the commonplace, you were laid in a manger between two sheep, which nuzzled you with their cold noses. As our eternal contemporary, we ask you to find your common people and give them an uncommon faith to be lifted on wings of delight into the glory of your grace. Teach them that "weeping may endure for a night, but joy comes in the morning" (Ps. 30:5 NKJV). Amen

Bibliography

Barclay, William. *The Gospel of John.* Vol. 2. Rev. Ed. Philadelphia: The Westminster Press, 1975.

Brown, Cohn. *Miracles and the Critical Mind.* Grand Rapids: Wm. B. Eerdmans Publishing Co., 1984.

Chappell, Clovis G. *Sermons from the Miracles.* New York: Abingdon Press, 1927.

Chawla, Navin. *Mother Teresa.* Rockport, Mass.: Element Books, Inc., 1996.

Cormier, Henri. *The Humor of Jesus.* New York: Alba House, 1977.

Darden, Robert. *Jesus Laughed, The Redemptive Power of Humor.* Nashville: Abingdon Press, 2008.

Hyers, Conrad. *And God Created Laughter, The Bible as Divine Comedy.* Atlanta: John Knox Press, 1987.

Laidlaw, John. *The Miracles of our Lord.* New York and Toronto: Funk and Wagnall's Co., 1892.

Lang, Cosmo Gordon. *The Miracles of Jesus.* London: Sir Isaac Pitman and Sons Ltd., 1910.

Macmillan, Hugh. *Our Lord's Three Raisings from the Dead.* London: Macmillan and Co., 1876.

Martin, James, SJ. *Between Heaven and Mirth, Why Joy, Humor, and Laughter Are at the Heart of the Spiritual Life.* New York: Harpers Collins Publishers, 2011.

Morgan, G. Campbell. *The Great Physician.* New York: Fleming H. Revell Co., 1937.

Palmer, Earl F. *The Humor of Jesus: Sources of Laughter in the Bible.* Vancouver, British Columbia: Regent College Publishing, 2001.

Richardson, Alan. *The Miracle-Stories of the Gospels.* London: SCM Press Ltd., 1941.

Rogers, Adrian. *Believe in Miracles but Trust in Jesus.* Wheaton, Illinois: Crossway Books, a Division of Good New Publishers, 1997.

Samra, Cal and Rose. *Holy Hilarity, Inspirational Wit and Cartoons.* Colorado Springs: Waterbrook Press, a division of Random House Inc., 1999.

Samra, Cal and Rose. *More Holy Hilarity, Inspirational Wit and Cartoons.* Colorado Springs: Waterbrook Press, a division of Random House Inc., 1999.

Samra, Cal and Rose. *Holy Humor, A Book of Inspirational Wit and Cartoons.* New York: Guideposts, 1996.

Samra, Cal and Rose. *More Holy Humor, Inspirational Wit and Cartoons.* New York: Guideposts, 1997.

Samra, Cal. *The Joyful Christ, The Healing Power of Humor.* New York: Harper and Row Publishers, Inc., 1986.

Shafto, G. R. H. *The Wonders of the Kingdom.* New York: George H. Doran Co., 1924.

Selby, Thomas G., and G. Milligan, J.G. Greenhough. *The Miracles of Jesus.* Cincinnati: Jennings and Graham, 1903.

Spurgeon, Charles H. *Sermons on the Miracles.* Greenwood, South Carolina: The Attic Press, Inc., 1977.

Straton, Hillyer Hawthorne. *Preaching the Miracles of Jesus.* Nashville: Parthenon Press, 1950.

Taylor, William M. *The Miracles of our Saviour.* Garden City, New York: Doubleday, Doran & Company, Inc., 1928.

Trench, Richard Chenevix. *Notes on the Miracles of our Lord.* Grand Rapids: Zondervan Publishing House, 1951.

Trueblood, Elton. *The Humor of Christ.* San Francisco: Harper and Row, Publishers, 1964.

Notes

Introduction

1. Alan Richardson, *The Miracle-Stories of the Gospels* (London: SCM Press Ltd., 1941), 46.
2. Hampton H. Sewell, 1874–1937, originally published in *Songs for Jesus*, 1925, quoted by Cal and Rose Samra, *Holy Humor, Inspiration Wit & Cartoons* (Portage, Mich.: "The Joyfulnoise Letter") 36.

Chapter One

3. Adrian Rogers, 1997, *Believe in Miracles but Trust in Jesus* (Wheaton: Crossway Books, A Division of Good News Publishers,1997), 12.
4. Richard Chenevix Trench, *Notes on the Miracles of Our Lord* (Grand Rapids: Zondervan Publishing House, 1951), 63.
5. Trench, 63.

6. Colin Brown, *Miracles and the Critical Mind* (Grand Rapids: Wm. B. Eerdmans Publishing Co., 1984), 113.
7. Richardson, 122.

Chapter Two

8. G. Campbell Morgan, *The Great Physician* (New York: Fleming H. Revell Co., 1937), 82.
9. William M. Taylor, *The Miracles of our Saviour* (New York: Doubleday, Doran & Company, Inc., 1928), 52.
10. Taylor, 54-55.

Chapter Five

11. Navin Chawla, *Mother Teresa: The Authorized Biography* (Rockport, Mass.: Element Books, Inc., 1966).
12. Chawla, 63.
13. Rogers,137.
14. Ibid.

Chapter Six

15. Taylor, 369.
16. William Barclay, *The Gospel of John, vol. 2,* rev. ed. (Philadelphia: The Westminster Press, 1975), 52.

Chapter Seven

17. G. R. H. Shafto, *The Wonders of the Kingdom* (New York: George H. Doran Co., 1924), 172.
18. Rogers, 174.

19. Ibid., 173.
20. Cal and Rose Samra, *Holy Humor, Inspirational Wit and Cartoons* (Portage, Mich.: "The Joyfulnoise Letter"), 17.

Chapter Nine

21. Martin, James, S. J., *Between Heaven and Mirth: Why Joy, Humor, and Laughter are at the Heart of the Spiritual Life* (New York: Harper Collins), 193–194.
22. Lois H. Morgan, quoted by Carl and Rose Samra, *Holy Humor, Inspirational Wit, and Cartoons,* 238-239. Used by permission.

Contact Information

To order additional copies of this book, please visit
www.redemption-press.com.
Also available on Amazon.com and BarnesandNoble.com
Or by calling toll free 1-844-2REDEEM.

CPSIA information can be obtained
at www.ICGtesting.com
Printed in the USA
BVHW030016060319
541875BV00001B/6/P